Living in America
TEACHER RESOURCE SERIES

Using Official Documents

New Readers Press

Developed originally by BOCES Geneseo Migrant Center with funding from a U.S. Education Department Office of Vocational and Adult Education, English Literacy and Civics Education Demonstration Grant.

BOCES Geneseo Migrant Center Project Developers:
Curriculum Developers:
  Karen Yamamoto,
  Jane Hogan, Ed.D
Contributors:
  Patricia Edwards
  Timothy J. Sparling
Graphic Designer:
  Eva McKendry

Special thanks to
  Robert E. Lynch, Director, BOCES Geneseo Migrant Center

Living in America Teacher's Resource Guide: Using Official Documents
ISBN 978-1-56420-527-8

Copyright © 2007 New Readers Press
New Readers Press
A Publishing Division of ProLiteracy
1320 Jamesville Avenue, Syracuse, New York 13210
www.newreaderspress.com

Printed in the United States of America
9 8 7 6 5 4 3

All proceeds from the sale of New Readers Press materials support literacy programs in the United States and worldwide.

Developmental Editor: Paula Schlusberg
Design and Production Manager: Andrea Woodbury
Production Specialist: Maryellen Casey
Cover Design: Kimbrly Koennecke

Contents

Introduction to the *Living in America* Curriculum

Welcome to *Living in America,* a curriculum tailored to the needs, interests, and language proficiency of literacy level adult English Language Learners (ELLs). Originally developed primarily for migrant farmworkers, the curriculum is now designed to address the needs of any ELL with very limited literacy and oral skills. **Effectiveness, efficiency,** and **relevance** are the hallmarks of the curriculum. *Living in America* provides a framework for successful learning, with concise, easy-to-follow directions and a selection of topics relevant to the situations and tasks that adult ELLs confront. The development of the curriculum was grounded in a series of learner-centered questions:

- What situations create problems for non-English-speaking adults?

- What life skills would make living in the U.S. easier for non-English-speaking adults?

- What vocabulary and conversation patterns would help facilitate daily communication?

- What civics information regarding legal issues would be pertinent to adult ELLs?

- What knowledge of rights and responsibilities would support community membership?

The design, materials, and strategies selected for the curriculum were guided by a set of instructor-centered questions:

- What lesson design and accompanying materials would best support instructors using the curriculum?

- What teaching strategies would be applicable to a variety of learners and suitable for the variety of instructional settings where those learners are taught?

The resulting curriculum, *Living in America,* provides literacy learners with functional, everyday language that is essential for successfully navigating a new community. Civics-based lessons paired with life-skill lessons help learners understand basic principles, customs, behaviors, and laws in the U.S. The combination of these lessons gives adult learners a voice and access to their rights and responsibilities as contributing community members.

The term "social civics" can be used for norms of expected behavior in situations where a behavior is inappropriate but not illegal. Behaviors and situations stressed in the curriculum are those which may be different from the norms and values in adult learners' native countries. Carefully selected vocabulary, statements, questions, and related dialogues develop learners' situational language skills, while the civics content fosters understanding and behaviors leading to improved community involvement and acceptance.

The most important force in motivating learners is the instructor's enthusiasm and investment in the curriculum. In *Living in America*, the instructor is the educational decision-maker. Decisions to modify, to reinforce, or to provide more practice are left for the instructor to make.

Approach to Language Learning

The *Living in America* curriculum incorporates an eclectic approach:

- **Communicative Language Instruction** emphasizes the language needed to communicate effectively
- **Total Physical Response** uses nonverbal means of communicating
- **Audio-lingual Instruction** provides the foundation for instructor-directed strategies to teach needed vocabulary and simple sentence patterns within exercises and dialogues

The curriculum focuses on oral competency and comprehension skills, so that learners are able to make their needs known and to understand the information given in response to their questions. Grammar is modeled in the curriculum but not explicitly explained. The curriculum takes the position that if a beginning speaker is understood, sentence form is not as important as the meaning conveyed. Integrating other ESL materials with the *Living in America* curriculum is encouraged and expected, especially to build prerequisite knowledge, including everyday vocabulary as well as letters, colors, dates, numbers, and times.

The Curriculum

Living in America consists of six teacher's resource guides (TRGs). Each TRG presents four to six units on thematically grouped topics. A list of the TRGs and the units in each is found at the end of this Introduction (p. 13). A unit contains two lessons, each designed to be approximately 120 to 180 minutes in length. The four to six instructional hours can be divided flexibly to meet learners' needs and the demands of the instructional setting.

Curriculum Features

Research-Based Strategies

- Model everything first
- Use gestures and body language
- Use realia or authentic materials
- Proceed in a clear instructional sequence: Oral Language → Reading → Writing
- Use a limited number of vocabulary words
- Use and practice vocabulary throughout the lesson
- Proceed from Instructor Model → Group Practice → Individual Practice
- Build on prior knowledge
- Give genuine, positive feedback
- Promote a learning environment that is cooperative, not competitive
- Use constant and consistent repetition and review
- Maintain high, yet reasonable expectations
- Focus on oral understanding and production of English

The curriculum embodies the following:

- **Life skills are paired with civics skills** for successful adjustment to living in and navigating the communities of the U.S.

- **Specific topics are nonsequential,** so that learners' needs and interests can guide topic selection

- **Lessons are adaptable** to any formal or informal learning environment and may be used with groups of various sizes

- **Listening and speaking are emphasized** to meet the needs of beginning learners, who may not be literate in their native languages

- **Research-based teaching strategies are woven** into all lesson activities and learner exercises (see sidebar)

- **A variety of learning styles is supported,** through cues supporting the needs of both visual and auditory learners, and through application activities supporting kinesthetic (hands-on) learners

- **Graphics, vocabulary cards, interactive activities, and activity sheets are included** to facilitate lesson planning and teaching

- **A civics introduction gives background information** about the legal principle supporting each civics lesson

Lesson Features

The lessons are designed to set learners up for success. Because of this, it is desirable to conduct lessons in English. Gestures, mime, drawings, and realia can be used to clarify and enhance understanding and learning. It is best to limit word-for-word translation from the learners' first language. Abstract concepts are an exception, since they are often difficult to comprehend without the support of a first language.

Each lesson includes:

- **Core vocabulary,** illustrated whenever possible and presented on cards

- **Scripted models** of dialogue patterns

- **Suggestions for support gestures and teacher remarks** for eliciting responses and giving praise

- **Model scripts** of oral lesson interactions, where I = Instructor, G = Group, and L = Learner
- **A patterned progression of activities** and repeated activity types to provide consistency for the learners and ease of delivery for the instructor

Lesson Components

Oral Language Activities: The life-skill and civic-responsibility lessons each contain four oral language activities. These begin with interactive vocabulary development, including opportunities for multiple repetition of each target word or phrase. Vocabulary is introduced in a consistent manner for each oral language activity.

Practice Exercises: In each oral language activity, there are practice exercises that incorporate review, enrichment, and application. These practice exercises either allow for cooperative learning or may involve concept development. All exercises model an example of teacher-student interaction and provide step-by-step instructions for easy reference.

Dialogues: Dialogues relate to the theme picture, storyboard, or lesson content. They model a simple conversation appropriate to the context of that lesson. Vocabulary and sentence patterns taught in the lesson are used in the dialogue, providing an opportunity for learners to practice short, focused conversations.

Comprehension Checks: The comprehension check at the end of an activity is a simple and efficient means of assessing whether the material and concepts have been learned. The checks are meant to be done quickly in order to establish whether there is a need for additional practice or whether the group should move forward in the lesson.

Skill Enhancements: Each lesson includes optional reading and writing activities. In reading activities, learners practice recognizing written forms of words or phrases within the context of the lesson. Whenever appropriate, writing activities provide an authentic task, so learners can practice writing something they can use later, like a list of emergency telephone numbers or a repair checklist.

Lesson Support Materials

Each *Living in America* TRG includes photocopy masters (PCMs) of graphics, vocabulary cards, interactive activities, and activity sheets needed to plan and teach lessons. A generic PCM with **OK/Not OK** cards is at the end of the book. In the units, each lesson includes a list of the PCMs needed for that lesson. These unit-specific PCMs follow the lesson notes for each unit. Some of the PCMs will be used multiple times in the lessons, and multiple sets of other PCMs will be needed for some activities. Therefore, copying or pasting them onto card stock or other heavy paper is advisable.

The lessons also include suggestions for realia or authentic materials to use in explaining or enhancing lesson content and activities. These suggestions include real or instructor-made documents, visuals from newspapers or magazines, and real objects.

Central Theme Picture and Storyboard: In each unit, the PCMs begin with a theme picture, introduced in Lesson A: Life Skill. This theme picture provides the context for the lesson. It can also be used to assess prior knowledge or provide a link to the learners' backgrounds. Lesson B: Civic Responsibility begins, when appropriate, with a storyboard of four frames, used primarily to demonstrate the civics concept under discussion. This storyboard is also often woven into the lesson itself.

Vocabulary Cards: In all lessons, large vocabulary cards include a graphic representation, or picture cue, and a target word or phrase to be presented simultaneously. Some lessons also include a set of small picture cards with just the graphic representation and a set of small word cards. The word is first taught orally. The print form becomes "environmental print" while the instructor refers to the graphic in the lessons. Learners may use the picture cues in all activities to provide support. Later in the lesson, the print forms of the words or phrases are the focus of the optional reading and writing activities.

Activity Sheets: Reproducible activity sheets are provided for selected activities and may be completed as a group or by individual learners. Most activity sheets are presented orally. They stress graphic representations rather than written words, to help learners succeed regardless of their reading level or ability. Teachers may want to create enlarged versions of activity sheets for ease in modeling or reviewing activities.

Unit Review Activities for Assessment: Each unit includes a review activity that can be used to assess and provide a written record of learner progress. These unit reviews mirror the kinds of exercises learners have done throughout the lessons. They combine the life skill and the civic responsibility being taught. The term *Review* is used rather than *Assessment* to minimize learners' test anxiety.

Selected Teaching Techniques

The *Living in America* curriculum uses language teaching techniques that research has shown to be appropriate for adult learners and effective with learners with limited or no prior exposure to English. The techniques suggested can be used with individuals or with groups of various sizes. They can also be modified for learners with more advanced abilities. Models and clear steps are provided within each activity to provide direction for instructors.

Assessment of Prior Knowledge: Prior knowledge is assessed at the beginning of each lesson using the theme picture or the storyboard. The instructor points to elements of the picture that represent key themes in the lesson and gives learners time to make associations, name or point out objects, and preview new words.

Introduction of Target Vocabulary: Target, or core, vocabulary is practiced in each oral language activity. New words or terms are learned in the context of the theme picture or storyboard. Graphic representations of words, available on the vocabulary cards, are also effective tools for introducing vocabulary. Mime and/or gestures are used to model actions, elicit responses, or explain complex concepts when new vocabulary is difficult to represent graphically.

Modeling: Instructors are provided with suggestions and examples of how to model vocabulary within the context of each lesson. Modeling accurate pronunciation and usage is important for beginning ELLs.

Repetition: Repetition is the key to helping language learners develop quick, natural responses. Activity and exercise guidelines suggest repeating every word, phrase, and sentence pattern three times, or more if necessary. Learners repeat target vocabulary as a group before individuals are asked to produce the vocabulary on their own.

Dialogues: Mini-dialogues and role plays of two to four sentences are introduced within activities. Longer dialogues are often introduced to present conversation patterns or to develop understanding of a civics concept.

Gestures: Use gestures to indicate when the learners should listen, respond, stop, wait, or take turns. Use gestures consistently to provide nonverbal cues during lessons.

Backward Buildup: This technique is employed by breaking a target sentence into parts and starting with repetition of the last phrase. For example: *I am going/ to the store/ to buy milk.* Teach *to buy milk* first. When the learner can say *to buy milk,* teach *to the store.* Combine the two. Then teach *I am going.* Finally, model the entire sentence and have the learners repeat it as one unit.

Substitution: Teach a target pattern, and then replace a word or phrase with another that completes the sentence. For example: *He is her husband.* After the learner can say this sentence, replace the initial target, *husband,* with *brother.* For example:

> **I:** "He is her husband."
> **I:** "Brother."
> **L:** "He is her brother."

Error Correction: Correct only when a learner's answer does not convey the correct meaning. State the correct response and ask the learner to restate the correct answer. For example, correct the error if the learner is asked to indicate that the windshield is broken, but responds with a reference to the tire.

> **I:** "What is broken?" (Point to windshield.)
> **L:** "The tire is broken."
> **I:** "Windshield. The windshield is broken." (Motion for the learner to repeat.)
> **L:** "The windshield is broken."

Modified Input: When the learner does not have the language facility to reproduce a complete sentence, speech can be modified by dropping articles, verbs, and inflectional endings. For example: *Windshield broken* or *Not OK.* With simplified grammar, the meaning is clearer to the learner. A learner's response in modified speech or using a one-word answer would not be corrected, as long as the correct meaning is conveyed.

Reinforcement: Give immediate and genuine reinforcement when a learner gives a correct answer. Use words like *good, good work, OK, yes, right,* and *terrific.* Restatement of a correct answer is also a form of positive reinforcement.

Preparation for Using *Living in America*

Prior to implementing the *Living in America* curriculum, familiarize yourself with the lesson content. Preview each lesson to make notes for quick reference and to gather or duplicate graphics, activity sheets, and additional materials needed for the lesson.

Many resources are available to instructors and learners in the field of ESL. Search local libraries or look on-line for materials that are appropriate for the level of ELLs being served and that contribute to professional development. A list of useful search topics is provided in the sidebar.

Useful Search Topics

- Adult Learners
- Civics Education
- EL-Civics
- English Language Learner (ELL)
- English as a Second Language (ESL)
- English for Speakers of Other Languages (ESOL)
- Immigrant Education
- Literacy
- Migrant Education
- ProLiteracy Worldwide
- Refugee Education
- Teaching English to Speakers of Other Languages (TESOL)

The *Living in America* Curriculum

Getting Along with Others
Introducing Yourself
Marking Your Calendar
Understanding Families
Protecting Yourself and Others
Understanding Manners in the U.S.

Using Official Documents
Using Money
Saving Necessary Documents
Finding Work
Preparing for Tax Time

Fitting into Your Community
Going to the Store
Recycling
Navigating the Community
Using the Phone
Paying for Phone Calls
Riding a Bicycle

Understanding Key Health Issues
Using Doctor and Hospital Services
Handling Dangerous Chemicals
Medicine and Controlled Substances
Having Safe Relationships

Operating a Motor Vehicle
Getting Ready to Drive
Driving
Owning a Car
Keeping Your Car Running
Maintaining Your Car
Navigating the Roads

Knowing Your Rights and Responsibilities
Getting a Lawyer
Communicating with the Neighbors and Police
Understanding Community Responsibilities
Understanding a Lease
Maintaining Housing

Unit 1

Using Money

Money Orders

VOCABULARY

NOUNS

Bank

Fee

Money order

Post office

ADJECTIVE

Safe

VERBS

Buy

Mail

Pay

Sign

Objective

To help learners understand that a money order is an alternative and safe method of payment to cash

Materials Included

- Central theme picture
- Large reproducible vocabulary cards
- Small reproducible picture cards
- Small reproducible word cards
- Box outline with pictures to make a die (dice)
- Buying and Using a Money Order activity sheet
- **Yes/No** cards
- **OK/Not OK** cards (page 180)

Materials Needed

- Additional instructor copy (enlarged) of the activity sheet
- Real or play money
- A pen
- Real or instructor-made mock-up of a money order
- Pictures of a post office and / or a bank (from magazines or other sources)
- Stamped and addressed envelope(s)

Central Theme Picture

MATERIALS

Theme picture

POSSIBLE RESPONSES

Mail

Man

Money order

Paper

Pen

Post office

Sign

Introduce Theme Picture

1. Show learners the theme picture and ask for a response.
2. Encourage learners to say anything about the picture that they can.

> **I:** "What's happening in this picture?" (Point out key things about the picture to elicit a response.)

Oral Language Activity 1

MATERIALS

Large noun cards

Box outline to make a die (dice)

Small picture cards for nouns (multiple sets)

Pictures of a post office and/or a bank

Introduce Target Nouns

1. Show each large noun card to the group while pronouncing each word slowly and clearly.

> **I:** "Bank." (Hold up the **bank** card and motion for the group to repeat the word together.)
> **G:** "Bank."
> **I:** "Good. Bank." (Hold up the **bank** card. Motion for the group to repeat.)
> **G:** "Bank."
> **I:** "Bank." (Motion for the group to repeat. Put the card at the front of the room.)
> **G:** "Bank."

2. Introduce all of the target nouns (**bank, fee, money order,** and **post office**) using the format above.
3. Use mime, realia, and pictures as necessary to help the group understand the target nouns.
4. Say each word and have the group repeat each one three times.
5. Repeat any words more than three times as necessary.

Picture Dice Activity

1. Cut and fold the box outline to make a die.
2. Prepare more than one die for a larger group so that the group can be split up or two dice can be rolled at once.
3. Have the group form a circle.
4. Demonstrate the activity by rolling the die (dice) and identifying the picture(s) that is (are) displayed faceup on it (them).
5. Have each learner take a turn around the circle to roll. Ask that learner to identify the picture that appears on the side of the die that is facing up.

> **I:** "OK. Roll. What's that?" (Motion for the learner that rolled the die to answer.)
>
> **L:** "Bank."
>
> **I:** "Good. OK. Next person." (Motion for the next person in the circle to roll and identify.)

NOTE

Instructor may need to make multiple sets of cards depending on the number of learners in the group. More than one copy of each card may be used, and more than two cards may be distributed to each learner.

Comprehension Check

1. Distribute vocabulary cards learned in Oral Language Activity 1 to the learners.
2. Make sure each learner has at least two different vocabulary cards.
3. Say a vocabulary word from Oral Language Activity 1. Have the learner with the corresponding card hold it up for the group and repeat the word.
4. Continue with other words until the group has practiced and checked their comprehension of all new vocabulary.

Oral Language Activity 2

Introduce Target Adjective and Verbs

1. Show each large adjective and verb card to the group while pronouncing each word slowly and clearly.

> **I:** "Safe." (Hold up the **safe** card and motion for the group to repeat the word together.)
>
> **G:** "Safe."
>
> **I:** "Good. Safe." (Hold up the **safe** card. Put a money order in a stamped and addressed envelope. Hold up the **OK** card.)
>
> **I:** "Safe." (Motion for the group to repeat.)
>
> **G:** "Safe."
>
> **I:** "Safe." (Point to the envelope with the money order. Place cash in an envelope. Hold up the **Not OK** card.)
>
> **I:** "Safe." (Point to the money order again. Motion for the group to repeat. Put the card at the front of the room.)
>
> **G:** "Safe."

2. Introduce the other target vocabulary using the format above.
3. Use mime and realia to demonstrate each verb (**buy, mail, pay, and sign**) and help the group understand the meaning of the target adjective and verbs.

MATERIALS

Large adjective card

Large verb cards

Large **money order** card (4 copies)

OK/Not OK cards

Suggested Mime and Realia to Accompany Phrases

Buy—show giving money in exchange for goods
Mail—show placing a money order in a stamped and addressed envelope and placing it in a mailbox
Pay—show using money order as payment for goods
Sign—show signing name to the money order prior to mailing it

4. Say each word and have the group repeat each one three times.
5. Repeat any words more than three times as necessary.

Money Order Activity

1. Put cards in sets according to the phrases indicated below. Hold up each set of cards for the group and ask the learners to repeat the phrases in the order indicated.

> **I:** "Buy money order." (Hold up both the **buy** and the **money order** cards. Mime buying a money order and motion for the group to repeat the phrase and gesture.)
>
> **G:** "Buy money order." (Learners should mime buying a money order.)
>
> **I:** "Sign money order." (Hold up both the **sign** and the **money order** cards. Mime signing a money order and motion for the group to repeat the phrase and gesture.)
>
> **G:** "Sign money order." (Mime signing a money order.)
>
> **I:** "Mail money order." (Hold up both the **mail** and the **money order** cards. Mime mailing a money order by mail, using an envelope, and motion for the group to repeat the phrase and gesture.)
>
> **G:** "Mail money order." (Mime mailing a money order.)

2. Repeat the method above with each combination at least three times.
3. Reshuffle the cards and motion for the learners to identify them verbally.
4. Demonstrate **safe** to refresh learners' understanding and have them repeat the term at least three times.
5. Have learners repeat each phrase, using gestures and realia that illustrate the concept (see suggestions on the following page).
6. Assist learners as necessary.

Suggested Gestures and Realia to Accompany Phrases

Buy money order—use play or real money to exchange for money order

Sign money order—gesture signing the money order

Mail money order—place the money order in a stamped and addressed envelope

Safe—place the money order in an envelope and associate the **OK** card with it; place cash in an envelope and associate the **Not OK** card with it to demonstrate what is not safe

Comprehension Check

1. Put together the sets of cards that form the phrases presented in Oral Language Activity 2. Place them on the table or in another visible location.
2. Use gestures to act out each phrase.
3. Ask learners to point to the sets of cards that correspond to the gesture made.
4. Demonstrate **safe** using the stamped and addressed envelope to mail a money order.
5. Check learner's understanding of **safe** by also showing cash being placed in a stamped and addressed envelope.
6. Ask learners to point to **safe** and to say which method (money order or cash by mail) is OK or Not OK.
7. Repeat several times to ensure comprehension of the target vocabulary and concept practiced in Oral Language Activity 2.

Oral Language Activity 3

MATERIALS

Large vocabulary cards

Yes/No cards

Review of Target Vocabulary

1. Review the vocabulary from Oral Language Activity 1 and Oral Language Activity 2 by showing each card or set of cards and motioning for a response.

> **I:** "What's this?" (Hold up the **money order** card. Motion for a response.)
> **G:** "Money order."
> **I:** "Good. Money order." (Hold up the **money order** card.)

2. State the correct term and gesture for the group to repeat the word or phrase to assist the learners.
3. Review all of the vocabulary terms, repeating them as necessary.
4. Assist learners as needed.

Concept Development Activity

1. Use the large noun, adjective, and verb cards to create sets as indicated in the list below.
2. Present the sets to the group in the order listed below to help learners understand the chronology of buying and using a money order.

Steps for Buying and Using a Money Order

Sets of cards
- Buy money order – bank – post office
- Pay fee
- Sign money order
- Mail money order

I: "Buy money order." (Hold up the **buy** and **money order** cards and motion for the group to repeat.)

G: "Buy money order."

I: "Bank. Post office." (Hold up the **bank** and **post office** cards and motion for the group to repeat.)

G: "Bank. Post office."

I: "Buy money order. Bank. Post office." (Hold up the **buy, money order, bank,** and **post office** cards and place them in a visible location in the order presented. Motion for the group to repeat.)

G: "Buy money order. Bank. Post office."

3. Place the cards in a visible location in the correct order, as presented above.
4. Complete the process of introducing each set of cards.
5. Shuffle the cards and distribute them to the group at random.
6. Assist the learners in working together to create the appropriate sets of cards, to place the sets in the correct order, and to say each phrase as a group.
7. Ask the learners to repeat each word or phrase to ensure verbal practice within the activity.

NOTE

For this check, the learners will need to understand and be able to distinguish the words Yes and No.

Comprehension Check

1. Collect the target noun, adjective, and verb cards and reshuffle them.
2. Introduce the cards in sets as shown in Oral Language Activity 3, identifying them correctly and incorrectly at random.
3. Model how to say Yes when the card is correctly identified, and No when it is incorrectly identified. Hold up the appropriate **Yes** or **No** card to reinforce the desired response.

> **I:** "Buy money order." (Hold up the **buy** and **money order** cards.)
>
> **I:** "Buy money order. Yes." (Point to the **buy** and **money order** cards and nod in agreement. Hold up the **Yes** card. Motion for the learners to repeat.)
>
> **G:** "Yes."
>
> **I:** "Pay fee." (Hold up the **buy** and **money order** cards again.)
>
> **I:** "Pay fee. No." (Point to the **buy** and **money order** cards and gesture disagreement. Hold up the **No** card. Motion for the learners to repeat.)
>
> **G:** "No."

4. Continue with other sets of target vocabulary at random.
5. Repeat words and phrases as necessary.

Oral Language Activity 4

Introduce the Couplet Activity

MATERIALS

Large vocabulary cards (multiple sets)

1. Write the couplets (question-answer sets, as in example below) on the board or on chart paper.
2. Refer to the couplets by pointing to each line and the corresponding cards as they are presented.

NOTE

Pointing to the couplets while reading is important to do even if the learners are nonreaders or nonliterate.

> **Speaker 1:** "What do you need to do?" (Hold up the set of cards that corresponds to the first step and motion for a response.)
>
> **Speaker 2:** "Buy money order."
>
> **Speaker 1:** "What do you need to do?" (Hold up the next set of cards and motion for a response.)
>
> **Speaker 2:** "Pay fee."
>
> **Speaker 1:** "What do you need to do?" (Hold up the next set of cards and motion for a response.)
>
> **Speaker 2:** "Sign money order."
>
> **Speaker 1:** "What do you need to do?" (Hold up the next set of cards and motion for a response.)
>
> **Speaker 2:** "Mail money order."

3. Make sure that the learners can respond to each set of cards before continuing on to the couplet activity.

Couplet Activity

NOTE

Multiple sets of cards will need to be provided.

1. Distribute sets of vocabulary cards among the group, providing each learner with at least one set.
2. Model the couplet activity by assisting the learners through the first couplet.

> **I:** "What do you need to do?" (Hold up the **buy** and **money order** cards and motion for a response. Learner(s) with the appropriate cards should respond verbally and hold up the **buy** and **money order** cards.)

3. Check which cards learners are holding and have the learner(s) with the **buy** and **money order** cards hold them up and repeat the phrase **buy money order.**
4. Continue with the activity by prompting the learners to respond verbally and to hold up the corresponding cards.

> **I:** "What do you need to do?" (Hold up the **pay** and **fee** cards and motion for a response.)
>
> **G:** "Pay fee." (Learners with the corresponding cards should respond verbally and hold up cards.)
>
> **I:** "What do you need to do?" (Hold up the **sign** and **money order** cards and motion for a response.)
>
> **G:** "Sign money order." (Learners should hold up cards.)
>
> **I:** "What do you need to do?" (Hold up the **mail** and **money order** cards and motion for a response.)
>
> **G:** "Mail money order." (Learners should hold up cards.)

5. Collect, shuffle, and redistribute the cards to the learners for more verbal practice.
6. Assist learners as needed.

Comprehension Check

1. Hold up two sets of cards and identify one set correctly.
2. Ask the learners to point to the correct set of cards.

> **I:** "Sign money order." (Hold up the **sign, money order, pay,** and **fee** cards.)
>
> **G:** "Sign money order." (Learners should point to the **sign** and **money order** cards.)

Reading Activity

MATERIALS

Large vocabulary cards

Small word cards

Small picture cards

Review

1. Shuffle all of the large target vocabulary cards.
2. Show each card to the group while pronouncing each word or term slowly and clearly.
3. Run a finger under each word or term to help learners begin to recognize the words or terms apart from the pictures.
4. Have the learners repeat the words and terms at least three times.

> **I:** "Post office." (Point to the term.)
>
> **G:** "Post office."
>
> **I:** "Post office." (Underline the term with a finger. Motion for the group to repeat it.)
>
> **G:** "Post office."

5. Continue to review with the cards using the pattern above.
6. Fold cards in half to show only the words and terms, to help learners become less dependent on the pictures.
7. Move from group to individual practice as learners become more comfortable reading the words and terms without the assistance of the pictures.

Concentration

1. Shuffle the small picture cards with the small word cards.
2. Spread cards out on a table facedown so that they are not overlapping.
3. Show learners how to do the activity by turning over two cards. If necessary, mark the backs of cards to be able to get a matched pair and an unmatched pair.
4. Read the cards or have the learners help read.
5. Model getting a matched pair to show how a player with a matched pair keeps the cards and is allowed an extra turn.
6. Model getting cards that do not match to show how the cards should be put back facedown on the table.
7. Motion for learners to begin the activity by choosing the first person to start.
8. Have each learner choose two cards and identify them verbally.
9. Assist learners as needed.
10. Have learners read aloud which pairs they collected when the activity is finished.
11. Motion for the learners to hold up the pairs to show the group as they read them.
12. Count each learner's pairs, and encourage the group to count along.

Writing Activity

MATERIALS

Large vocabulary cards

Buying and Using a Money Order activity sheet (one enlarged and one per learner)

Review

1. Shuffle all of the target vocabulary cards.
2. Show each card to the group while pronouncing each word slowly and clearly.

3. Run a finger under each word to help learners begin to recognize the words apart from the pictures.
4. Have the learners repeat the words at least three times.

> **I:** "Money order." (Point to the term.)
> **G:** "Money order."
> **I:** "Money order." (Underline the term with a finger. Motion for the group to repeat the word.)
> **G:** "Money order."

NOTE

Separating words from pictures should be done gradually and after plenty of practice.

5. Continue to review with the cards using the pattern above.
6. Fold cards in half to show only the words and terms, to help learners become less dependent on the pictures.
7. Move from group to individual practice as learners become more comfortable reading the words and terms without the assistance of the pictures.

Buying and Using a Money Order Activity

1. Place an enlarged Buying and Using a Money Order activity sheet on the board or other visible surface.
2. Put a set of large vocabulary cards in a visible location.
3. Distribute an activity sheet to each learner.
4. Demonstrate to the group how to look at the pictures and write the corresponding terms.
5. Have learners repeat the steps for buying and using a money order after the activity sheet has been completed.
6. Assist learners as necessary.

Steps for Buying and Using a Money Order

- Buy money order – bank – post office
- Pay fee
- Sign money order
- Mail money order

Lesson B – Civic Responsibility

Paying Bills

VOCABULARY

NOUNS
Electric bill
Gas bill
Rent
Telephone bill
Water bill

ADJECTIVES
Early
Late
On time

VERB
Shut off

Objectives
- To help learners understand the importance of paying bills
- To help learners focus on the importance of paying bills on time

Materials Included
- Large reproducible vocabulary cards
- Small reproducible picture cards
- Pay Bills by Money Order activity board
- Circle the Correct Word activity sheet
- Pay the Bills activity sheet
- **No** card
- **OK/Not OK** cards (page 180)

Materials Needed
- Die (dice) or coins to use as counters
- Place markers, one per learner (buttons, coins, dried beans, paper clips, etc.)
- Magazine pictures of household appliances, apartments, houses, and *for rent* signs
- Real or instructor-made mock-ups of utility and rent bills
- Additional instructor copy (enlarged) of the activity sheets
- Real or toy telephones
- Rental agreements
- Maps
- Clock or picture of a clock
- Calendar or mock-up of calendar pages

Civics Introduction

Paying Bills

Currency should never be sent through the U.S. or international mail services. It is unsafe to send cash by mail because it can easily get lost or stolen, and it cannot be traced to a specific person or transaction.

The safest method for making payments by mail is to send a check or money order. Money orders can be reported stolen; and damaged, lost, or stolen money orders can be replaced. When a money order is purchased through the U.S. Postal Office Service, it does not have an expiration date, so it can be cashed at any time. A money order may be made out for payment to any person or company, or it can be made out to more than one person. The money order can be mailed safely, allowing it to circulate as easily as cash. The person receiving a money order can cash it at any post office or financial institution. For security reasons, the person cashing a money order must show identification in order to receive the money. To send money outside the U.S., international money orders can be purchased in any post office in amounts up to $700. For use within the U.S., money orders can be purchased in amounts up to $1,000, with a daily limit of $10,000 per customer. Individuals who purchase money orders in amounts totaling more than $3,000 must show a government-issued or state-issued picture ID.[1]

This topic is of special importance to non-English-speaking adults, particularly newly arrived ones, because they may not have savings or checking accounts at U.S. banks. For making payments by mail, money orders are a safe choice because they can be cancelled or traced if necessary. Additionally, money orders are equal to cash, as the money is guaranteed to the recipient, and there is no wait time for having them processed.

[1]http://www.usps.com/money/sendingmoney/moneyorders/welcome.htm
(viewed 9/13/05)

Oral Language Activity 1

MATERIALS

Large noun cards

Real or instructor-made mock-ups of utility and rent bills

Real or toy telephones

Magazine pictures

Introduce Target Nouns

1. Show each large noun card to the group while pronouncing each word or term slowly and clearly.

> **I:** "Electric bill." (Hold up the **electric bill** card. Point to items that would be included in an electric bill. Motion for the group to repeat the term together.)
>
> **G:** "Electric bill."
>
> **I:** "Good. Electric bill." (Hold up the **electric bill** card. Motion for the learners to repeat.)
>
> **G:** "Electric bill."
>
> **I:** "Electric bill." (Motion for the group to repeat. Put the card at the front of the room.)
>
> **G:** "Electric bill."

2. Introduce the target nouns (**gas bill, rent, telephone bill,** and **water bill**) using the format above.

3. Use mime and realia as necessary to help the group understand the target nouns (see suggestions below).

Suggestions for Realia

> **Electric bill**—real or mock-up of an electric bill, pictures or other representations of what might contribute to the cost on the electric bill (lighting, electrical appliances, computer equipment, etc.)
>
> **Gas bill**—real or mock-up of a gas bill, pictures or other representations of what might contribute to the cost on the gas bill (gas oven/stove, heater/furnace)
>
> **Rent**—picture(s) of apartments, real or mock–ups of housing and rental agreements with the cost per month or per week highlighted
>
> **Telephone bill**—real or mock-up of a telephone bill, map to use in showing how long-distance calls can increase charges, real or toy telephones
>
> **Water bill**—real or mock-up of a water bill, pictures or other representations of what might contribute to the cost on the water bill (sink, shower, bathtub, washing machine, garden hose, dishwasher, etc.)

4. Say each word or term and have the group repeat each one three times.

5. Repeat any words more than three times as necessary.

Find the Bill Activity

1. Shuffle the noun cards and place them in different locations around the room.

2. Distribute realia to the learners, making sure each individual has at least one piece of realia.

3. Have learners search the room for the large noun cards that correspond to the realia they are holding.
4. Ask the learners to identify the nouns verbally as they are located.

> **I:** "OK. What's this?" (Hold up a water bill and motion for a response.)
>
> **G:** "Water bill."
>
> **I:** "Good." (Search for the **water bill** card in the room.)
>
> **I:** "Water bill." (Hold up both the **water bill** card and the water bill once the card is located. Motion for the group to repeat.)
>
> **G:** "Water bill."

5. Motion for learners to begin searching the room for cards that correspond to the realia that each learner holds.

Comprehension Check

1. Hold up each target noun card for the group.
2. Introduce the cards one by one, identifying them correctly and incorrectly at random.
3. Model how to say Yes when the card is correctly identified and No when it is incorrectly identified.

> **I:** "Electric bill." (Hold up the **electric bill** card.)
>
> **I:** "Electric bill. Yes." (Point to the **electric bill** card and nod in agreement. Motion for the learners to repeat.)
>
> **G:** "Yes."
>
> **I:** "Water bill." (Hold up the **electric bill** card again.)
>
> **I:** "Water bill. No." (Point to the **electric bill** card and gesture disagreement. Motion for the learners to repeat.)
>
> **G:** "No."

4. Continue with other noun cards at random.
5. Repeat words as necessary.

Oral Language Activity 2

MATERIALS

Large verb card

Small adjective and noun picture cards (multiple sets)

OK/Not OK cards (one set per learner)

No card

Real clock or picture of clock

A calendar

Magazine pictures

NOTE

For this activity, learners will need to have an understanding of dates. Review dates and names of months as necessary. For the purpose of this activity, three late payments or non-payments will result in services being shut off.

Introduce Target Adjectives and Verb

1. Show each large adjective and verb card to the group while pronouncing each word slowly and clearly.

> **I:** "Early." (Hold up the **early** card. Motion for the group to repeat together.)
>
> **G:** "Early."
>
> **I:** "Good. Early" (Hold up the **early** card. Motion for the group to repeat.)
>
> **G:** "Early."
>
> **I:** "Early." (Put the card at the front of the room. Motion for the group to repeat.)
>
> **G:** "Early."

2. Introduce the other target adjectives and the verb **(late, on time,** and **shut off)** using the format above.
3. Use mime and realia as necessary to help the group understand the target terms.

Suggestions for Mime and Realia

Early—use a clock to demonstrate **early** by focusing on the scheduled time for beginning the class and showing when **early** would be; use a calendar to demonstrate **early** for a certain day or date

Late—use a clock to demonstrate **late** by using the scheduled time for beginning the class and showing when **late** would be; use a calendar to demonstrate **late** for a certain day or date

On time—use a clock and a calendar to show **on time** (at the exact time or on the exact day)

Shut off—use lights in the room or an appliance or machine to demonstrate **shut off;** use bills, calendars, and the lights or machines to help learners understand that **shutting off** might be a result of not paying bills or paying them late

4. Say each word and have the group repeat each one three times.
5. Repeat any words more than three times as necessary.

Pay Bills Activity

1. Make multiple sets of the small noun picture cards and place them in a pile facedown in the center of the group.
2. Make multiple sets of the small adjective picture cards and place them in a second pile facedown.
3. Introduce the group to the concept of **paying bills early, on time, late,** or **not paying** (using the **No** card).
4. Associate the **OK** card with **paying bills early** and **on time** and the **Not OK** card with **paying bills late** or **not paying.**

5. Show learners that paying bills late or not at all may result in services being shut off.
6. Demonstrate to the learners that the purpose of the activity is to draw two cards, one from each pile, and identify them verbally, showing them to the group.
7. Model by drawing a card from the bill pile and then from the adjective pile, using the format below, with cards and identifications given as examples.

> **I:** "Gas bill." (Draw the **gas bill** card and identify it for the group.)
>
> **I:** "On time." (Draw the **on time** card and identify it for the group.)
>
> **First L:** "Electric bill." (Learner draws the **electric bill** card and identifies it for the group.)
>
> **First L:** "Late." (Learner draws the **late** card and identifies it for the group.)
>
> **Second L:** "Water bill." (Learner draws the **water bill** card and identifies it for the group.)
>
> **Second L:** "Early." (Learner draws the **early** card and identifies it for the group.)
>
> **Third L:** "Rent." (Learner draws the **rent** card and identifies it for the group.)
>
> **Third L:** "No." (Learner draws the **No** card and identifies it for the group.)

8. Ask learners to hold all of the cards drawn. Once three **late** or nonpayment **(No)** cards are collected by the same learner, he or she will receive the **shut off** card to signify an end of services.

Comprehension Check

1. Distribute **OK** and **Not OK** cards to each learner.
2. Hold up various combinations of cards and ask the learners to classify them as OK or Not OK.

> **I:** "Electric bill. On time." (Hold up appropriate cards. Motion for a response.)
>
> **G:** "OK." (Learners should hold up the **OK** card.)
>
> **I:** "Gas bill. No." (Hold up appropriate cards. Motion for a response.)
>
> **G:** "Not OK." (Learners should hold up the **Not OK** card.)

Suggested Combinations

- Electric bill/on time
- Gas bill/late
- Rent/No
- Telephone bill/early

- Electric bill/late
- Water bill/early
- Rent/on time
- Telephone bill/No

Oral Language Activity 3

© New Readers Press. All rights reserved.

MATERIALS

Large vocabulary cards (from Lessons A & B)

Pay Bills by Money Order activity board

Die (dice) or coins to use as counters

Place markers, one per learner (buttons, coins, dried beans, paper clips, etc.)

Small picture cards (multiple sets of select terms from Lessons A & B)

NOTE

When using a coin as a counter, heads = move two spaces and tails = move one space.

This activity can be a contest or game. Have learners keep the cards they draw from the center. The learner with the most **early** or **on time** cards is the winner.

Review Target Vocabulary

1. Review the vocabulary from Lesson A and Lesson B by showing the cards in sets previously practiced or as individual cards and motioning for a response.

> **I:** "What's this?" (Hold up the **buy** and **money order** cards. Motion for a response.)
>
> **G:** "Buy money order."
>
> **I:** "Good. Buy money order." (Hold up the **buy** and **money order** cards.)

2. State the correct term, and gesture for the group to repeat the phrase or word when learners need assistance.
3. Review all of the vocabulary cards and repeat words or phrases as necessary.

Pay Bills by Money Order Activity

1. Make multiple sets of small picture cards from Lesson B **(early, late, on time,** and **shut off)** and the **No** card. Shuffle them together, placing them facedown in the center of the activity board.
2. Put place markers on **Start** on the activity board.
3. Give the die (dice) or coin to a learner to begin the game. Use the format below, with identifications given as examples.

> **I:** "OK. Please start." (Motion for the learner to roll the die or flip the coin.)
>
> **I:** "Great. Move three spaces." (Guide the learner to the correct space on the board. Motion for the learner to identify the picture.)
>
> **L:** "Electric bill."
>
> **I:** "Good job." (Motion for the next learner to take a turn.)

4. Have learners take turns moving around the board and identifying vocabulary verbally.

5. Ask learners to draw a card from the center pile when they land on a square that directs them to pay a specific bill.
6. Motion for the learner to decide if the **early, late, on time, No,** or **shut off card** is OK or Not OK, assisting them as necessary.

Comprehension Check

1. Shuffle all of the large vocabulary cards together and place them faceup on a table or other visible surface.
2. Call out a term. Ask learners to locate the corresponding card and pick it up from the surface where it is displayed.
3. Have the learner who locates the card first identify it verbally for the group.
4. Continue with other terms until all of the cards have been collected and identified.
5. Repeat the check as necessary to ensure that all learners have a solid understanding of the vocabulary.

Oral Language Activity 4

MATERIALS

Large vocabulary cards

Real or mock-ups of utility bills

Introduce the Dialogue

1. Write the dialogue (see example below) on the board or other visible surface.
2. Refer to the dialogue by pointing to each line and holding up the corresponding cards as the dialogue is presented.
3. Model the dialogue for learners.

NOTE

Pointing to the dialogue while reading is important to do even if the learners are nonreaders or nonliterate.

Speaker 1:	"What do you need to do?" (Hold up the **electric bill** card and motion for a response.)
Speaker 2:	"Pay electric bill."
Speaker 1:	"What do you need to do?" (Hold up the **buy** and **money order** cards and motion for a response.)
Speaker 2:	"Buy money order."
Speaker 1:	"What do you need to do?" (Hold up the **sign** and **money order** cards and motion for a response.)
Speaker 2:	"Sign money order."
Speaker 1:	"What do you need to do?" (Hold up the **mail** and **money order** cards and motion for a response.)
Speaker 2:	"Mail money order."

4. Substitute a different bill in the first question-and-answer set of the dialogue.
5. Make sure that the learners can respond to each phrase card before continuing on to the dialogue activity.

Dialogue Activity

1. Model the dialogue by assisting the learners through the first couplet.

> **I:** "What do you need to do?" (Hold up the **pay** and **electric bill** cards. Motion for a response.)
>
> **G:** "Pay electric bill."

2. Ask learners to respond using the verbal and visual prompts given.
3. Continue with the activity by using the appropriate sets of cards to prompt the learners to respond verbally.

> **I:** "What do you need to do?" (Hold up the **buy** and **money order** cards and motion for the learners to respond.)
>
> **G:** "Buy money order."
>
> **I:** "What do you need to do?" (Hold up the **sign** and **money order** cards and motion for the learners to respond.)
>
> **G:** "Sign money order."
>
> **I:** "What do you need to do?" (Hold up the **mail** and **money order** cards and motion for the learners to respond.)
>
> **G:** "Mail money order."

4. Practice the dialogue using other bills that need to be paid to vary the dialogue.
5. For additional, more advanced practice, go through the dialogue again, using realia or pictures to prompt learners to identify the bill that needs to be paid. For example, hold up a picture of a lamp or other electrical appliance, a shower, a phone, a house or apartment, a furnace, etc.
6. Assist the group as necessary.

Comprehension Check

1. Hold up realia or pictures combined with various kinds of bills represented by the noun cards.
2. Ask learners if the match is OK (accurate) or Not OK (inaccurate).

> **I:** "OK?" (Hold up a **water bill** card and a picture of a sink. Motion for a response.)
>
> **G:** "OK."
>
> **I:** "OK?" (Hold up a **water bill** card and picture of a lamp. Motion for a response.)
>
> **G:** "Not OK."

Reading Activity

MATERIALS

Large vocabulary cards

Circle the Correct Word activity sheet (one enlarged and one per learner)

NOTE

Separating words from pictures should be done gradually and after plenty of practice.

Review

1. Shuffle all of the target vocabulary cards.
2. Show each card to the group while pronouncing each word slowly and clearly.
3. Run a finger under each word to help learners begin to recognize the words apart from the pictures.
4. Have the learners repeat the words at least three times.

> **I:** "Electric bill." (Point to the term.)
> **G:** "Electric bill."
> **I:** "Electric bill." (Underline the term with a finger. Motion for the group to repeat it.)
> **G:** "Electric bill."

5. Continue to review with the cards, using the pattern above.
6. Fold cards in half to show only the words and terms, to help learners become less dependent on the pictures.
7. Move from group to individual practice as learners become more comfortable reading the words and terms without the assistance of the pictures.

Circle the Correct Word Activity

1. Place a set of large vocabulary cards on the board or in another visible location.
2. Distribute a Circle the Correct Word activity sheet to each learner.
3. Post an enlarged version of the activity sheet on the wall or other available surface.
4. Ask learners to look at and identify each picture.
5. Help learners to use the large vocabulary cards to match a picture to one of the words listed next to the picture.
6. Show learners how to circle the word that corresponds to the picture.
7. Assist learners as necessary.

Writing Activity

MATERIALS

Large vocabulary cards

Pay the Bills activity sheet (one enlarged and one per learner)

Review

1. Shuffle all of the target vocabulary cards together.
2. Show each card to the group while pronouncing each word slowly and clearly.
3. Run a finger under each word to help learners begin to recognize the words apart from the pictures.

4. Have the learners repeat the words at least three times.

> **I:** "Rent." (Point to the word.)
> **G:** "Rent."
> **I:** "Rent." (Underline the word with a finger. Motion for the group to repeat the word.)
> **G:** "Rent."

5. Continue to review with the cards, using the pattern above.
6. Fold cards in half to show only the words, to help learners become less dependent on the pictures.
7. Move from group to individual practice as learners become more comfortable reading the words without the assistance of the pictures.

Pay the Bills Activity

1. Post the large noun and verb combinations on the board or in another visible location.
2. Place an enlarged Pay the Bills activity sheet on the board or other visible surface.
3. Distribute an activity sheet to each learner.
4. Show the group how to look at the pictures on the activity sheet and use the cards placed in the room for assistance in identifying the required phrase.
5. Use the example on the enlarged activity sheet to show learners how to write the correct words on the lines.
6. Have learners complete their own sheets.
7. Assist learners as necessary.

Unit Review Activity

MATERIALS

Unit Review activity sheet (one enlarged and one per learner)

Vocabulary cards (from Lesson B)

Large **Safe** card (from Lesson A)

NOTE

The Unit Review Activity can be done as a group activity for reinforcing the concepts learned in the lesson or done as an individual activity for assessment purposes.

Review Activities

1. Use the vocabulary cards, including the **safe** card, to review the vocabulary and concepts of the unit.
2. Distribute a copy of the Unit Review activity sheet to each learner. Post an enlarged copy of the activity sheet in the front of the room.
3. Ask learners to complete the three activities. Review the different directions for each activity on the sheet. If necessary, use the enlarged activity sheet to help learners identify the information in each activity and understand how to answer each one.

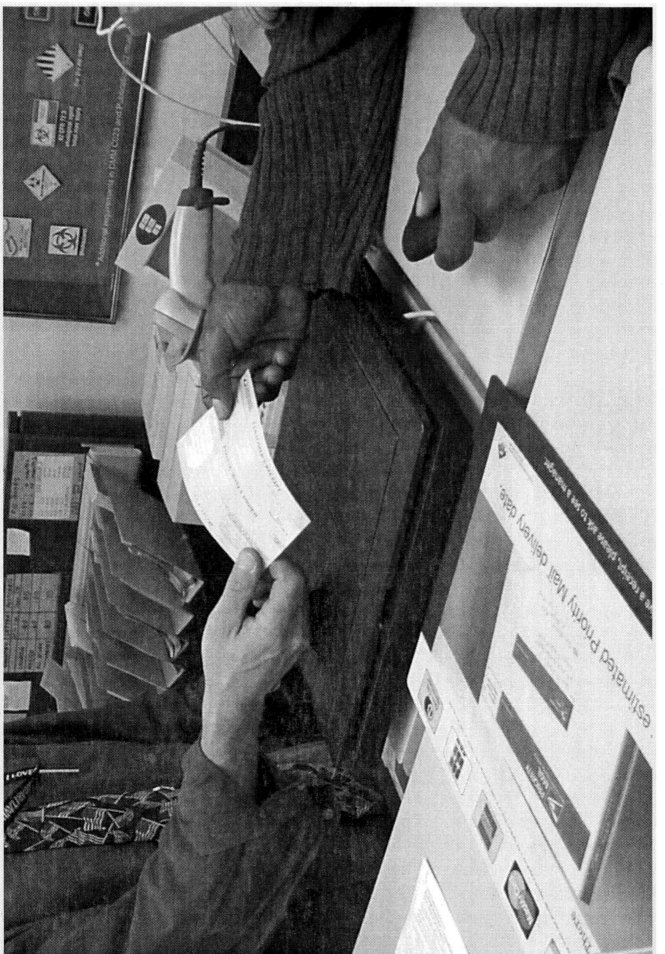

Unit 1 *Using Money*

37

Bank

Fee

Post office

Unit 1 *Using Money* Lesson A *Life Skill*

Money order

Large Vocabulary Cards

Unit 1 *Using Money* Lesson A *Life Skill*

Safe

✂ -

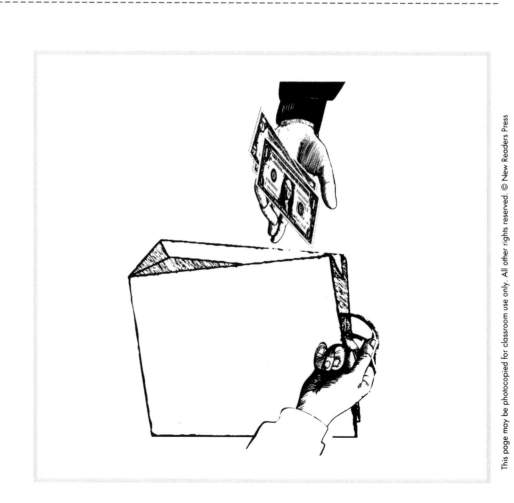

Buy

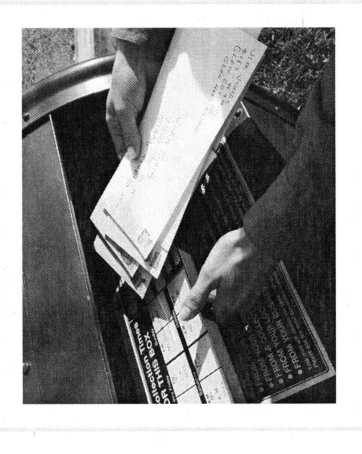

Mail

Unit 1 *Using Money* Lesson A *Life Skill*

✂

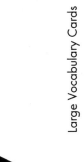

Pay

Unit 1 *Using Money* Lesson A *Life Skill*

Sign

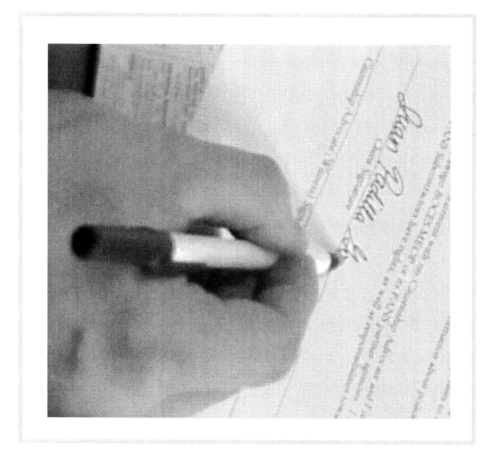

No

Yes

Unit 1 *Using Money:* A   Small Picture Cards

Unit 1 *Using Money:* A   Small Picture Cards

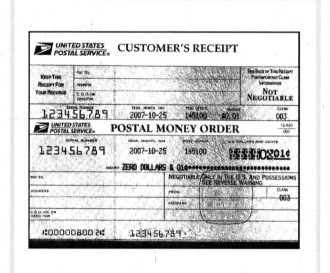

Unit 1 *Using Money:* A   Small Picture Cards

Unit 1 *Using Money:* A   Small Picture Cards

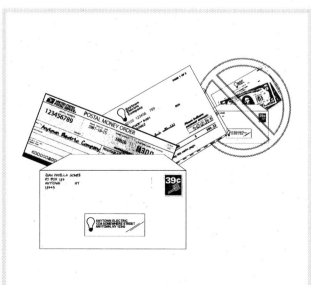

Unit 1 *Using Money:* A   Small Picture Cards

Unit 1 *Using Money:* A   Small Picture Cards

Unit 1 *Using Money:* A Small Picture Cards

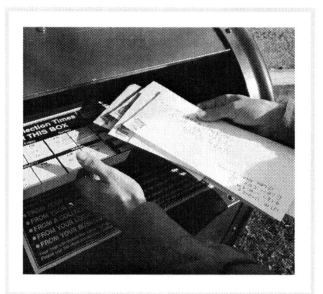

Unit 1 *Using Money:* A Small Picture Cards

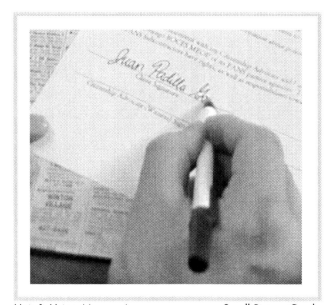

Unit 1 *Using Money:* A Small Picture Cards

Sign

Unit 1 *Using Money:* A Small Word Cards

Pay

Unit 1 *Using Money:* A Small Word Cards

Mail

Unit 1 *Using Money:* A Small Word Cards

Bank

Fee

Money order

Post office

Safe

Buy

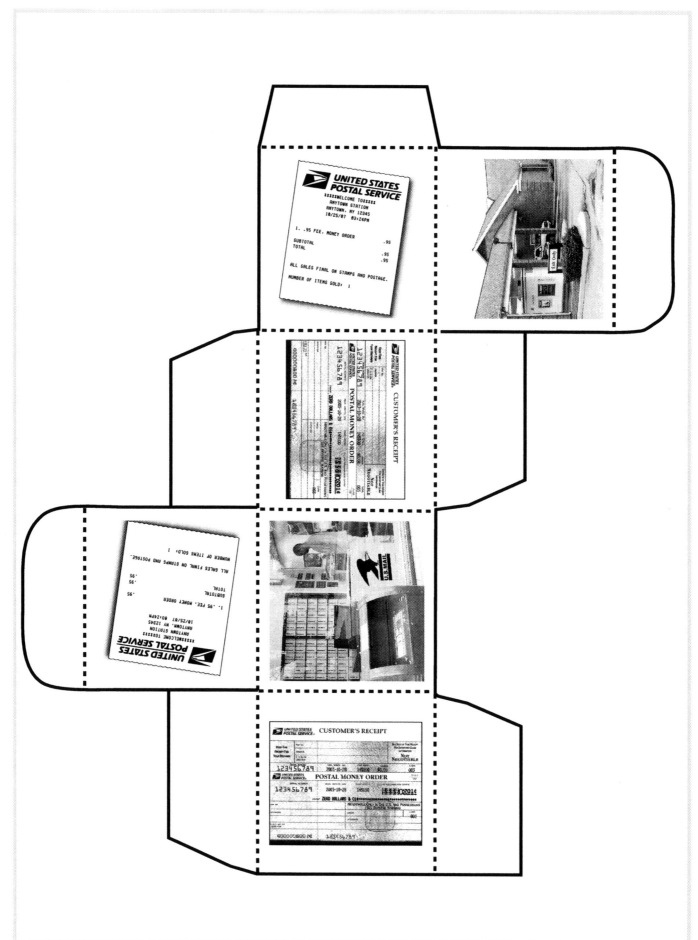

Buying and Using a Money Order Activity

Look at the pictures. Write the words on the lines. Create the steps for buying
and using a money order.

1.

_____

2.

_____

3.

_____

4.

_____

Unit 1 _Using Money_ Lesson A _Life Skill_

Writing Activity Sheet

Electric bill

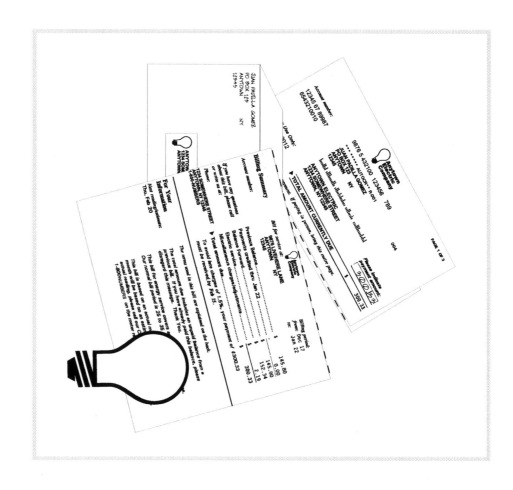

Gas bill

Telephone bill

Large Vocabulary Cards

Rent

Large Vocabulary Cards

Water bill

✂ -

Early

On time

Late

Shut off

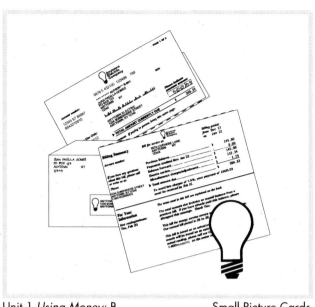

Unit 1 *Using Money*: B · Small Picture Cards

Unit 1 *Using Money*: B · Small Picture Cards

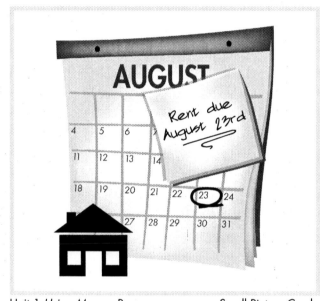

Unit 1 *Using Money*: B · Small Picture Cards

Unit 1 *Using Money*: B · Small Picture Cards

Unit 1 *Using Money*: B · Small Picture Cards

Unit 1 *Using Money*: B · Small Picture Cards

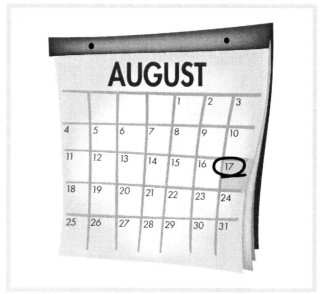

Unit 1 *Using Money:* B   Small Picture Cards

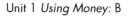
Unit 1 *Using Money:* B   Small Picture Cards

Unit 1 *Using Money:* B   Small Picture Cards

Using Money

Unit 1 *Using Money* Lesson B *Civic Responsibility*

Circle the Correct Word Activity

Look at each picture. Circle the correct word.

1.   Gas bill   Electric bill   Rent

2.   Gas bill   Telephone bill   Water bill

3.   Water bill   Electric bill   Rent

4.   Rent   Telephone bill   Gas bill

5.   Water bill   Rent   Electric bill

Unit 1 *Using Money* Lesson B *Civic Responsibility*

Reading Activity Sheet

Pay the Bills Activity

Look at each picture. Write the correct words on the lines.

1.

_____ _____

2.

_____ _____

3.

_____ _____

4.

_____ _____

Unit 1 *Using Money* Lesson B *Civic Responsibility*   Writing Activity Sheet

Circle the safe method for sending money by mail.

Look at the picture combinations. Check OK or Not OK.

OK   Not OK

1.

_____   _____

2.

_____   _____

3.

_____   _____

Circle Yes or No for the following situation.

Yes No

Unit 2

Saving Necessary Documents

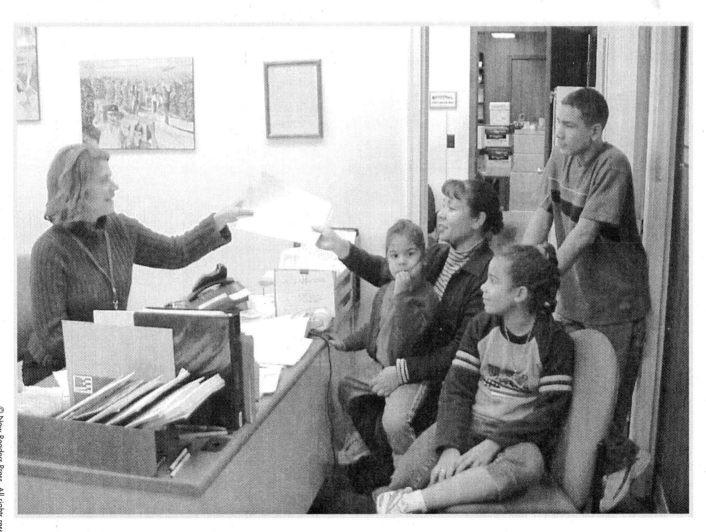

Important Papers

VOCABULARY

NOUNS
Birth certificate
Driver's license
Paid bill
Papers
Pay stub
Social Security card

ADJECTIVE
Important

VERBS
Carry
Save
Show

QUESTION/ANSWERS
Do you have a _____?
Yes, I have a_____.
No, I don't have a _____.

NOTE
If real (or copied) documents are used, ensure that personal identification does not become public. Teach learners to keep personal identification secure.

Objective
To enable learners to identify the important papers or documents people must save and the ones they must carry with them

Materials Included
- Central theme picture
- Large reproducible vocabulary cards
- Small reproducible word cards
- Write the Document Names activity sheet
- **Yes/No** cards

Materials Needed
- Additional instructor copy (enlarged) of the activity sheet
- A large envelope marked **Important**
- One large envelope per learner
- Real documents (or instructor-made mock-ups), including pay stubs, paid bill receipts, Social Security card(s), driver's license(s), and birth certificate(s)
- A waste basket or trash bag
- Junk mail, newspaper circulars, wrinkled lined paper, or other unimportant papers
- A wallet or a purse

Central Theme Picture

Introduce Theme Picture

1. Show learners the theme picture and ask for a response.
2. Encourage learners to say anything about the picture that they can.

> **I:** "What's happening in this picture?" (Point out key things about the picture to elicit a response.)

Oral Language Activity 1

Introduce Target Nouns

1. Show each vocabulary card to the group while pronouncing each word slowly and clearly.

> **I:** "Birth certificate." (Hold up a real or replica birth certificate. Hold up the **birth certificate** card. Motion for the group to repeat together.)
> **G:** "Birth certificate."
> **I:** "Good. Birth certificate." (Motion for the group to repeat together.)
> **G:** "Birth certificate."
> **I:** "Birth certificate." (Motion for learners to repeat. Put the card at the front of the room.)

2. Model the pronunciation of all the nouns.
3. Say each word and have the group repeat each one three times.
4. Review the noun cards again in a random order. Pronounce each word and have learners repeat, to give more verbal practice.

Concentration

1. Shuffle two sets of large vocabulary cards and place them facedown on the table.
2. Show learners how to play by turning over two cards.
3. Have the group identify each card verbally.
4. Model getting a matched pair to show how a player with a matched pair keeps the cards and is allowed an extra turn.
5. Model getting cards that do not match to show how the cards should be put back facedown on the table.
6. Motion for learners to begin.
7. Assist learners as necessary.
8. Count each learner's pairs and encourage the class to count along to determine the winner.

NOTE

The learner with the most pairs wins. If desired, learners can be divided into teams to play the game. In that case, a learner from each team alternately takes a turn. The team with the most pairs wins.

Comprehension Check

1. Collect the target noun cards and reshuffle them.
2. Introduce the cards one by one, identifying them correctly and incorrectly at random.
3. Model how to say Yes when the card is correctly identified, and No when it is incorrectly identified. Hold up the appropriate **Yes** or **No** card to reinforce the desired response.

> **I:** "Birth certificate." (Hold up the **birth certificate** card.)
>
> **I:** "Birth certificate. Yes." (Point to the **birth certificate** card and nod in agreement. Motion for the learners to repeat.)
>
> **G:** "Yes."
>
> **I:** "Pay stub." (Hold up the **birth certificate** card again.)
>
> **I:** "Pay stub. No." (Point to the **birth certificate** card and motion disagreement. Ask the learners to repeat.)
>
> **G:** "No."

4. Continue with other nouns at random.
5. Repeat words as necessary.

Oral Language Activity 2

Introduce Target Adjective

1. Put a stack of important documents and a pile of other papers that are not important (circulars from the paper, junk mail, wrinkled lined paper, etc.) on the table or other available surface.
2. Model putting each important document in the large envelope.

> **I:** "Important." (Place each document in the envelope and say *important*.)

3. Give an important document to a learner.
4. Gesture for the learner to put the important document in the envelope while saying *important*.

> **I:** "Important." (Gesture for the learner to repeat.)
>
> **L:** "Important."
>
> **I:** "Important." (Motion for the whole group to repeat.)
>
> **G:** "Important."
>
> **I:** "Important." (Motion for the group to repeat.)
>
> **G:** "Important."

5. Collect the unimportant items from the table.
6. Hold up each item for the group.

> **I:** "Important. No." (Hold up one of the unimportant
> items and put it in the wastebasket. Motion for the
> group to repeat together.)
>
> **G:** "Important. No."
>
> **I:** "Important. No." (Hold up the **No** card. Motion for the
> group to repeat together.)
>
> **G:** "Important. No."
>
> **I:** "Important. No." (Motion for learners to repeat. Put the
> unimportant item in the wastebasket.)
>
> **G:** "Important. No."

NOTE

The **save** card from Unit 3 can also be used here.

7. Mime saving an important document by carefully putting it in the envelope. Introduce the term **save** to the group using the method above.

8. Combine **save** with target nouns and ask the group to repeat each phrase at least three times.

> **I:** "Save the pay stub." (Hold up the pay stub. Put it in the
> envelope. Motion for the group to repeat.)
>
> **G:** "Save the pay stub."
>
> **I:** "Save the pay stub." (Motion for each learner to repeat
> individually.)
>
> **L:** "Save the pay stub."
>
> **I:** "Save the pay stub." (Motion for the whole group to repeat.)
>
> **G:** "Save the pay stub."

9. Repeat the phrase, substituting each document and using the method above.

Important Documents Activity

1. Write the word **save** on the envelope marked **important.**
2. Put all the important documents and the envelope marked **save—important** in front of the learners.
3. Hold up the envelope marked **save—important,** choose an important document, and model placing it in the envelope.

> **I:** "Save the pay stub."(Motion for the group to repeat.)
>
> **G:** "Save the pay stub."
>
> **I:** "Save the pay stub." (Motion for each learner to repeat
> individually.)
>
> **L:** "Save the pay stub."
>
> **I:** "Save the pay stub." (Motion to pairs or small groups of
> learners to respond in unison.)
>
> **G:** "Save the pay stub."

4. Continue putting important documents into the **save—important** envelope.
5. Have learners repeat the phrase (**save** + document name) using other important documents (such as the birth certificate and paid bill).
6. Distribute important documents (either large vocabulary cards, actual documents, or instructor-made mock-ups) to the group.
7. Motion for learners to add each important document to the envelope.
8. Have learners repeat the phrase (**save** + document name) with each important document as it is added to the envelope.

Comprehension Check

1. Give each learner a set of **Yes** and **No** cards.
2. Hold up a document which should be saved. Model holding up the **Yes** card to indicate that it is important.

> **I:** "Important? Yes? No?" (Hold up a birth certificate. Identify it. Hold up the **Yes** card.)
>
> **I:** "Birth certificate. Important. Yes." (Motion for learners to repeat.)

3. Repeat with a paper document that is not important. Hold up the paper. Follow the pattern above. Model holding up the **No** card.
4. Continue asking the learners to identify important documents and unimportant items using the **Yes** and **No** cards.
5. Repeat the Comprehension Check using the verb **save.** First use documents and papers that learners need to save.

> **I:** "Save? Yes? No?" (Hold up a paid bill. Hold up the **Yes** card.)

6. Then use documents that are not important and ask learners if each should be saved.

> **I:** "Save? Yes? No?" (Hold up wrinkled paper. Hold up the **No** card.)

Oral Language Activity 3

MATERIALS

Large noun cards

Theme picture

Envelopes (one for each learner)

Yes/No cards (one set per learner)

A wallet or a purse

Real or instructor-made mock-ups of important documents (multiple copies)

NOTE

The meaning of **carry** in this activity is to have a document that is normally carried, as in to carry a license or carry an ID.

Introduce Target Verbs

1. Hold up the theme picture and point to the woman showing the papers.

> **I:** "Show the papers." (Mime showing various documents to the learners.)
>
> **I:** "Show the papers. Show." (Motion for the learners to repeat.)
>
> **G:** "Show."
>
> **I:** "Good. Show." (Hold up a document and mime the verb **show.** Motion for the learners to repeat.)
>
> **G:** "Show."

2. Make sure the learners repeat the word three times.
3. Combine the verb **show** with the target nouns and use them to prompt the learners.

> **I:** "Show the birth certificate." (Hold up the birth certificate. Motion for the group to repeat.)
>
> **G:** "Show the birth certificate."
>
> **I:** "Show the birth certificate." (Motion for learners to repeat the term individually.)
>
> **L:** "Show the birth certificate."
>
> **I:** "Show the birth certificate." (Motion for the group to repeat.)
>
> **G:** "Show the birth certificate."

4. Go through each target noun and practice with the verb **show.**
5. Introduce **carry** by using documents normally carried in pockets, wallets, or purses to demonstrate the meaning of the verb.
6. Put the objects on the table or other available surface and one at a time put them away in a purse, wallet, or pocket.

> **I:** "Carry driver's license." (Hold up a driver's license and put it away in a wallet or purse.)
>
> **I:** "Carry driver's license." (Motion for the learners to repeat.)
>
> **G:** "Carry driver's license."
>
> **I:** "Carry driver's license." (Repeat the action of putting the driver's license away and carrying it. Motion for the learners to repeat.)
>
> **G:** "Carry driver's license."

7. Continue to mime the meaning of **carry** by taking each document out of a wallet or purse and then putting it back.
8. Combine the verb **carry** with the target nouns.
9. Have learners repeat each phrase three times.

Total Physical Response (TPR)

1. Hold up the **paid bill** card.
2. Hold up a real paid bill (or instructor-made mock-up) and signal for the learners to answer.

> **I:** "Paid bill." (Point to the word **paid** marked on the bill. Motion for the learners to repeat.)
>
> **G:** "Paid bill."
>
> **I:** "Save paid bill." (Motion for the learners to repeat.)
>
> **G:** "Save paid bill."
>
> **I:** "Save paid bill." (Model saving the paid bill by putting the document in the **save—important** envelope.)

3. Pass out documents or large noun cards to the learners, making sure that each person has a birth certificate, a pay stub, a driver's license, a Social Security card, and a paid bill.
4. Repeat the format above, using each document.

> **I:** "Save pay stub." (Motion for learners to repeat and do the action. Model saving the pay stub.)
>
> **G:** "Save pay stub." (Learners should repeat the phrase and act out saving the pay stub by placing the document in an envelope.)

5. Demonstrate and practice each action (**show, carry,** and **save).**
6. Have the learners repeat and act out each phrase using the instructor-provided realia or vocabulary cards.

Comprehension Check

1. Distribute a set of **Yes** and **No** cards to each learner.
2. Demonstrate each verb correctly and incorrectly at random.
3. Have the learners decide if the verb is being demonstrated correctly. Have learners demonstrate by holding up the **Yes** card or the **No** card and saying the correct word.

> **I:** "Save the paid bill."
>
> **I:** "Save the paid bill. Yes." (Place the paid bill in an envelope. Hold up the **Yes** card. Motion for the group to repeat.)
>
> **G:** "Yes." (Learners should hold up the **Yes** card.)
>
> **I:** "Save the paid bill." (Hold up the paid bill. Throw it in the wastebasket. Hold up the **No** card and motion for the group to repeat.)
>
> **G:** "No." (Learners should hold up the **No** card.)

4. Continue with other verb and noun combinations to make sure that the group understands the meaning of each term.

NOTE

Pointing to the word while reading is important to do even if the learners are nonreaders or nonliterate.

Oral Language Activity 4

MATERIALS

Large noun cards

Yes/No cards

Real or instructor-made replicas of important documents (multiple copies)

NOTE

Pointing to the words while reading is important to do even if the learners are non-readers or nonliterate.

Introduce Question/Answer Forms

1. Show each vocabulary card to the learners. Motion for learners to identify the card.
2. Place each card on the table or other available surface so that each card can be seen clearly. Do not overlap or crowd the cards together.
3. Write the questions and answers on the board or other visible surface.
4. Introduce the Question/Answer forms to the learners by pronouncing the words slowly and clearly, pointing to each word as you say it. Follow the example below. Have the learners repeat each line.

> **I:** "Do you have a birth certificate?" (Hold up the **birth certificate** card and motion for the learners to repeat.)
>
> **G:** "Do you have a birth certificate?"
>
> **I:** "Do you have a birth certificate?" (Point to each word. Motion for the learners to repeat.)
>
> **G:** "Do you have a birth certificate?"
>
> **I:** "Do you have a birth certificate?" (Hold up the **birth certificate** card and motion for the learners to repeat.)
>
> **G:** "Do you have a birth certificate?"

5. Have learners repeat the question three times.
6. Practice the question form with the name of each of the other documents.
7. Point to the answer forms on the board. Introduce each one to the learners by pronouncing the words slowly and clearly, pointing to each word as you say it. Follow the example below. Have learners repeat each line.

> **I:** "Yes, I have a birth certificate." (Hold up the **birth certificate** card. Nod in agreement while looking at the card. Motion for the learners to repeat.)
>
> **G:** "Yes, I have a birth certificate."

8. Have learners repeat the answer three times.
9. Include the negative response by writing it on the board or other available surface.
10. Use the **birth certificate** card and the **No** card to assist the learners.

> **I:** "No, I don't have a birth certificate." (Mime looking for the birth certificate. Shake head to indicate disagreement. Have the learners repeat.)
>
> **G:** "No, I don't have a birth certificate."

11. Have learners repeat the answer three times.
12. Practice the answer forms with the name of each of the other documents.

Question and Answer Activity

1. Prompt the learners by holding up each target noun card.
2. Identify each noun, and help learners form the question using each noun.
3. If necessary, assist learners by writing the questions and answers on the board or on chart paper.

> **I:** "Birth certificate." (Hold up the **birth certificate** card and motion for the learners to respond.)
> **G:** "Birth certificate."
> **I:** "Do you have a birth certificate?" (Motion for the learners to repeat. Prompt learners by pointing to the written question.)
> **G:** "Do you have a birth certificate?"
> **I:** "Yes, I have a birth certificate." (Hold up the **birth certificate** card and the **Yes** card. Motion for the learners to repeat.)
> **G:** "Yes, I have a birth certificate."
> **I:** "No, I don't have a birth certificate." (Hold up the **No** card. Motion for the learners to repeat.)
> **G:** "No, I don't have a birth certificate."

4. Repeat the activity with each of the target noun cards.
5. Motion for each learner to ask the question.
6. Have each learner answer based on the noun card.

Comprehension Check

1. Distribute various documents to the learners.

Suggested Documents

Birth certificate	Driver's license
Pay stub	Social Security card
Paid bill	

2. Make sure that each learner has a document.
3. Ask the learners at random which documents they hold. Follow the examples on the next page.

> **I:** "Olga, do you have a birth certificate?" (Point to the birth certificate held by the learner.)
>
> **L:** "Yes, I have a birth certificate." (Learner should hold up the birth certificate.)
>
> **I:** "Kevin, do you have a driver's license?" (Point to the Social Security card held by the learner.)
>
> **L:** "No, I don't have a driver's license." (Learner should hold up a Social Security card.)

4. Assist learners as necessary.

Reading Activity

Review

MATERIALS

Large noun cards

Small word cards (multiple sets, if necessary)

Envelope marked **save—important**

1. Shuffle all of the noun cards together.
2. Show each card to the group while pronouncing each word slowly and clearly.
3. Run a finger under each word to help learners begin to recognize the words apart from the pictures.
4. Have the learners repeat the nouns at least three times.

> **I:** "Pay stub." (Point to the term.)
>
> **G:** "Pay stub."
>
> **I:** "Pay stub." (Underline the term with a finger. Motion for the group to repeat the term.)
>
> **G:** "Pay stub."

NOTE

Separating words from pictures should be done gradually and after plenty of practice.

5. Continue to review with the cards, using the pattern above.
6. Fold cards in half to show only the words, to help learners become less dependent on the pictures.
7. Move from group to individual practice as learners become more comfortable reading the words without the assistance of the pictures.

NOTE

When learners have difficulty identifying a card, have them place it to the side. At the end of the activity, go back to that card and have the learners identify it. Prompt learners as necessary by saying the word aloud and having learners repeat.

Saving the Documents Activity

1. Place all of the target noun cards on the table or other visible surface for the group to use as a reference.
2. Place the small word cards faceup on the table or other available surface. Make sure there is at least one card for each learner.
3. Have each learner select a word card and identify it verbally.
4. Assist learners in identifying each card correctly.
5. Motion for learners to place the identified cards in the **save—important** envelope or in a purse or wallet.

Writing Activity

Large noun cards

Write the Document Names activity sheet (one enlarged and one per learner)

Review

1. Shuffle all of the noun cards together.
2. Show each card to the group while pronouncing each word slowly and clearly.
3. Run a finger under each word to help learners begin to recognize the words apart from the pictures.
4. Have learners repeat the nouns at least three times.

> **I:** "Pay stub." (Point to the term.)
> **G:** "Pay stub."
> **I:** "Pay stub." (Underline the term with a finger. Motion for the group to repeat the term.)
> **G:** "Pay stub."

5. Continue to review with the cards, using the pattern above.
6. Fold cards in half to show only the words, to help learners become less dependent on the pictures.
7. Move from group to individual practice as learners become more comfortable reading the words without the assistance of the pictures.

Write the Document Names Activity

1. Distribute a Write the Document Names activity sheet to each learner.
2. Place the enlarged activity sheet in a visible location.
3. Place the large vocabulary cards in the front of the room for learners to use as a reference.
4. On the enlarged sheet, point to each picture and have the group identify each one verbally.
5. Demonstrate to the learners how to trace over each word as it is read aloud.
6. Point to the corresponding picture and have the group repeat the term.
7. Demonstrate on the enlarged sheet how to write the words on the lines provided.
8. Have the learners write each word next to the picture and traced word on the line provided on their own sheets.

NOTE

Separating words from pictures should be done gradually and after plenty of practice.

Lesson B – Civic Responsibility

Requirements for School

VOCABULARY

NOUNS
Children
Health record
Immunizations
Physical exam
School

VERBS
Have
Need

SENTENCES
You need a _____.

Objectives
- To help learners understand that a parent must keep a health record for each child and that it must contain a record of immunizations
- To ensure that learners understand that children must have a birth certificate, a health record with immunizations, and a physical examination to be able to go to school

Materials Included
- Storyboard
- Central theme picture (from Lesson A)
- Large reproducible vocabulary cards
- Small reproducible word cards
- **Yes/No** cards
- **OK/Not OK** cards (page 180)
- School Checklist activity sheet

Materials Needed
- Additional instructor copy (enlarged) of the activity sheet
- A health record book, physical exam form, and school enrollment form (or copies or instructor-made mock-ups)
- Large envelopes (one per learner)
- Props, including a toy stethoscope (or other items typical of a doctor), a pen, a map, a coat, a hat, an umbrella, and a pair of sunglasses
- Magazine pictures of a grocery store, an airplane, and food items

Civics Introduction

Requirements for School Enrollment

Immunizations are required for school-age children to prevent the spread of communicable diseases such as mumps, measles, rubella, German measles, pertussis (whooping cough), diphtheria, tetanus (lockjaw), influenza type B, chicken pox, and hepatitis B.

States vary in their immunization requirements for school-age children. For example, the law in New York lists the specific set of immunizations required for children to attend any school in the state. The law also states that children cannot be in school for more than 14 days without receiving the required immunizations. The school must receive a certificate showing that the child has received the required immunizations.[1] It is important for parents to be aware of immunization requirements, as they vary from state to state and are under constant revision. Children who have not met state immunization requirements beyond the deadline established by the state will be excluded from school attendance by either the school principal or the leading school official.

This topic is of special importance to newly arrived non-English-speaking adults who want to ensure that their children can attend school. They need to understand that, as part of the process of enrolling children for school in the U.S., it is necessary for parents to bring a birth certificate and a health record to the school. The health record indicates the date of a recent physical examination as well as dates reflecting all of the immunizations required by the state in which the family resides.

[1]http://www.health.state.ny.us/prevention/immunzation/docs/2164.pdf (viewed 9/13/05)

Storyboard Activity

Introduce Storyboard

1. Introduce the storyboard sequence to the group.
2. Place the storyboard in a visible place.
3. Ask the learners to identify what they see in each frame. Encourage them to say anything about each picture that they can.
4. Point to each frame and make the following statements:

> **Frame 1:** The mother and children are at school.
> **Frame 2:** The school needs important papers.
> **Frame 3:** The mother shows the birth certificates and health records.
> **Frame 4:** The children go to school.

5. Repeat the sentences that accompany the storyboard at least three times.

Oral Language Activity 1

MATERIALS

Large noun cards (from Lessons A and B)

Props, including an official health record, a physical exam form, and a toy stethoscope or other items typical of a doctor

Storyboard

Yes/No cards (one set per learner)

Introduce Target Nouns

1. Hold up each noun card from Lesson B and have the group repeat each word.
2. Show each card to the group, pronouncing each word slowly and clearly.

> **I:** "Children." (Hold up the **children** card and point to the children in the storyboard. Indicate that the word refers to the whole group. Motion for the learners to repeat.)
> **G:** "Children."
> **I:** "Good. Children." (Motion for learners to repeat together.)
> **G:** "Children."
> **I:** "Very good. What's this?" (Point to the children in the storyboard. Motion for a response.)
> **G:** "Children."

3. Introduce the word **child.** Use the pattern above but point to one child at a time in the picture.
4. Introduce the other noun cards (**health record, immunizations, physical exam,** and **school**) using the method above.

5. Introduce the term **health record** using an official health record (or a copy or mock-up) and the vocabulary card. Use appropriate props to mime a physical exam by taking a pulse, looking in a learner's ear, and/or using a toy stethoscope.
6. Have all learners repeat each term three times.
7. Review target nouns from Lesson A before continuing on to the next activity.

NOTE

The team with the most cards wins.

Picture Race

1. Display all of the noun cards from Lessons A and B at one end of the room (either on the table or in another visible place).
2. Divide the group into two teams. (In the case of a small group, individual learners can be their own teams.)
3. Have the teams line up on either side of the table, facing the place where the cards are displayed.
4. Call out each term and have two learners, one from each team, race to retrieve the corresponding noun card that was called.
5. Have the first person who reaches the card pick up the card and say the word to the group.
6. Say the words again and have the learners repeat them as necessary.
7. Note any cards that are difficult for the group. At the end of the activity, take those cards and have learners repeat them again.

NOTE

For this activity, learners will need to understand and be able to distinguish between the words Yes and No.

Comprehension Check

1. Give each learner a set of the **Yes** and **No** cards.
2. Point to a large vocabulary card and say the corresponding word. Motion for a response.

> **I:** "School." (Point to the **school** card. Motion for a response.)
> **G:** "Yes." (Learners should hold up the **Yes** card.)

3. Point to a picture and say a word that does not correspond to the picture.

> **I:** "Children." (Point to the **school** card. Motion for a response.)
> **G:** "No." (Learners should hold up the **No** card.)

4. Review all of the target vocabulary for Lesson B. Identify cards correctly or incorrectly at random.
5. Repeat the process using vocabulary from Lesson A as review.

Oral Language Activity 2

MATERIALS

Large vocabulary cards (multiple sets; see list in Pick a Card activity, page 76, step 10)

Real or instructor-made mock-ups of documents (birth certificate, health record, and physical exam record)

A large envelope

Props, including a pen, a map, a coat, a hat, an umbrella, and sunglasses

Magazine pictures of a grocery store, food items, and an airplane

Introduce Verbs

1. Put the documents in the envelope and take them out of the envelope one by one. Use the large vocabulary cards to reinforce meaning.
2. Stress the verb **have** each time a document is taken out of the envelope.

> **I:** "I have a health record. Have." (Take out the health record. Hold up the **health record** card. Place stress on the verb **have.)**
>
> **I:** "Have." (Motion for the group to repeat.)
>
> **G:** "Have."
>
> **I:** "Good. Have." (Motion for the group to repeat.)
>
> **G:** "Have."
>
> **I:** "Have." (Motion for the group to repeat. Put the card at the front of the room.)
>
> **G:** "Have."

3. Practice the concept of **have** with each document.
4. Repeat the pattern above using the verb **need.**
5. Mime different situations where **need** could be understood by the learners. Use the example situations below.

Example Situations

> • Looking for a pen—I **need** a pen to write my name.
> • Showing two faraway points on a map—I **need** to take an airplane.
> • Going to the store—I **need** money to buy food.
> • Showing pictures of examples of extreme weather—I **need** a coat, a hat, an umbrella, or sunglasses.

> **I:** "I need a health record. Need." (Look for the **health record** card. Stress the verb **need.)**
>
> **I:** "Need." (Motion for learners to repeat.)
>
> **G:** "Need."
>
> **I:** "Good. Need." (Motion for the group to repeat.)
>
> **G:** "Need."
>
> **I:** "Need." (Motion for the group to repeat.)
>
> **G:** "Need."

6. Have learners use the verbs **need** and **have** with the items needed for school enrollment. Use pictures, large vocabulary cards, and real or mock-ups of documents.

Items Needed for School Enrollment

• Health record	• Immunizations
• Physical exam	• Birth certificate

Pick-a-Card Activity

1. Shuffle two (or more) sets of cards from Lessons A and B together.

Example Cards

Birth certificate	Physical examination
School	Children
Health record	Immunizations
Social Security card	Driver's license

2. Deal out the cards so that each player has four cards.
3. Deal a hand to include the instructor if there are enough cards.
4. Put the rest of the cards facedown in a pile in the middle of the group on an available surface.
5. Place a set of large vocabulary cards from Lessons A and B in a visible location for learners to use as reference and demonstrate the activity to the group.
6. Write a model on the board or on chart paper and read through it slowly, pointing to each word.

> **I:** "I need a health record. Do you have a health record?" (Point to the **health record** card displayed in a visible location.)
>
> **L:** "Yes, I have a health record." (Learner should pass the **health record** card to the person who requested it.)
> **or**
> **L:** "No, I don't have a health record."

7. Help the learners remember the pattern when necessary by repeating the model above.
8. In the front of the room or in some other visible location, place the vocabulary cards of the items needed for school enrollment so that students can use them to check if they have the proper cards to win.
9. Model the activity using the pattern above. Identify a card that is needed for school enrollment and that is not a card currently held.

NOTE

Each player can only hold four cards at a time. When the learner who is asked does not have the requested card, he or she must draw a card from the pile of cards in the middle. If the card that is drawn is not needed, it should be placed at the bottom of the pile. If the card drawn is needed, the learner must discard a different card he or she is holding.

10. Have learners ask for the cards they need for school enrollment **(birth certificate, health record, immunizations,** and **physical exam).**
11. Continue until a learner holds the correct set of the four cards for items needed for school enrollment.
12. Assist learners as necessary.

Comprehension Check

1. Give each learner a set of large vocabulary cards (from Lessons A and B). Each learner should have two or more different cards.
2. Say the question and sentence patterns with each term. Ask learners to repeat and hold up the corresponding cards.

> **I:** "I need a physical exam." (Motion for the learner(s) with the card to hold it up and repeat.)
>
> **L:** "I need a physical exam." (Learner(s) with the card should hold up the **physical exam** card.)
>
> **I:** "Do you have a birth certificate?" (Motion for the learner(s) with the card to hold it up and repeat.)
>
> **L:** "Do you have a birth certificate?" (Learner(s) should hold up the **birth certificate** card.)

Oral Language Activity 3

MATERIALS

Large vocabulary cards (from Lessons A & B)

Envelope marked **save—important**

OK/Not OK cards (one set per learner)

Introduce the Concept Development Activity

1. Hold up the envelope marked **save—important.**
2. Place the **health record** and the **birth certificate** cards in the large envelope and motion for learners to say the words **save** and **important.**
3. Hold up the **immunizations** and **children** cards.

> **I:** "Children need immunizations." (Hold up the **immunizations** and **children** cards.)
>
> **I:** "Children need immunizations." (Point to the **immunizations** card. Motion for the learners to repeat.)
>
> **G:** "Children need immunizations."
>
> **I:** "Good. Children need immunizations." (Motion for learners to repeat together.)
>
> **G:** "Children need immunizations."
>
> **I:** "Very good. What do children need?" (Point to the **immunizations** card. Motion for a response.)
>
> **G:** "Children need immunizations."

4. Repeat the previous steps, substituting the term **physical exam.**
5. Hold up the envelope marked **save—important.**
6. Take out and hold up the **health record** card and motion for a response.

> **I:** "Save the health record." (Put the **health record** card in the envelope. Motion for the learners to repeat.)
>
> **G:** "Save the health record."

7. Have learners repeat the phrase at least three times. Take the **health record** card out so that it is available for the next part of the activity.
8. Mime giving immunizations to one or more learners in the room.

> **I:** "Immunizations." (Post the **immunizations** card on the board or on chart paper. Write a date next to the **immunizations** card.)
>
> **I:** "A health record has immunizations." (Mime giving an immunization to a learner. Write the date next to the **immunizations** card. Motion for the group to repeat.)
>
> **G:** "A health record has immunizations."
>
> **I:** "A health record has immunizations." (Motion for the group to repeat.)
>
> **G:** "A health record has immunizations." Put the cards for **health record** and **immunizations** together.
>
> **I:** "A health record has immunizations." (Motion for the group to repeat.)
>
> **G:** "A health record has immunizations."

9. Hold up the physical examination form and the **physical exam** card. Place the form in a visible location and post the card on the board or on chart paper.

> **I:** "Physical exam." (Point to the **physical exam** card. Write a date next to the **physical exam** card.)
>
> **I:** "A health record has a physical exam." (Point to the **health record** and **physical exam** cards. Motion for the group to repeat.)
>
> **G:** "A health record has a physical exam."
>
> **I:** "A health record has a physical exam." (Motion for the group to repeat.)
>
> **G:** "A health record has a physical exam."
>
> **I:** "A health record has a physical exam." (Put the cards for **health record** and **physical exam** together. Motion for the group to repeat.)
>
> **G:** "A health record has a physical exam."

Concept Development Activity

1. Hold up the **school** card and the **OK** card and place them side by side at the front of the room.

> **I:** "Schools need a health record with immunizations." (Hold up the **health record** and **immunizations** cards and point to the **school** card.)
>
> **I:** "... with immunizations." (Hold up the **immunizations** card. Place the **immunizations** card under the **school** card. Leave enough space between them for another card. Motion for the group to repeat.)
>
> **G:** "... with immunizations." (Learners should point to the **immunizations** card.)
>
> **I:** "... a health record." (Put the **health record** card between the **school** card and the **immunizations** card. Motion for the learners to repeat.)
>
> **G:** "... a health record." (Learners should point to the **health record** card.)
>
> **I:** "... a health record with immunizations." (Point to the **health record** and **immunizations** cards. Motion for the learners to repeat.)
>
> **G:** "... a health record with immunizations." (Learners should point to the **health record** and **immunizations** cards.)
>
> **I:** "Schools need ..." (Point to the **school** card. Motion for the group to repeat.)
>
> **G:** "Schools need ..." (Learners should point to the **school** card.)
>
> **I:** "... a health record with immunizations." (Point to the **health record** and **immunizations** cards. Motion for the learners to repeat.)
>
> **G:** "... a health record with immunizations." (Learners should point to the **health record** and **immunizations** cards.)

2. Point to the **OK** card and model the complete sentence, asking the learners to repeat it.

> **I:** "Schools need a health record with immunizations." (Point to the **health record** and **immunizations** cards and point to the **school** card. Motion for the learners to repeat.)
>
> **G:** "Schools need a health record with immunizations."

3. Have the group repeat the entire sentence at least three times.
4. Substitute the **physical exam** card for the **immunizations** card and model the sentence for the group.

> **I:** "Schools need a health record with a physical exam."
> (Point to the **health record** and **physical exam** cards and point to the **school** card. Motion for the learners to repeat.)
>
> **G:** "Schools need a health record with a physical exam."

5. Use the backward build-up method modeled above if the group has difficulty producing the entire sentence using **physical exam.**

6. Remove all of the cards from the board or other surface.

7. Hold up each item that is needed for school enrollment and have the group repeat each sentence to ensure their understanding of the concept.

> **I:** "Schools need a birth certificate." (Place the **school** card on the board or other visible surface. Put the **birth certificate** card under the **school** card. Hold up the **OK** card and motion for the group to repeat.)
>
> **G:** "Schools need a birth certificate. (Learners should point to the **school** and **birth certificate** cards.)
>
> **I:** "Schools need a health record." (Place the **health record** card under the **birth certificate** card. Point to the **OK** card and motion for the group to repeat.
>
> **G:** "Schools need a health record." (Learners should point to the **school** and **health record** cards.)

8. Hold up the **immunizations** and **physical exam** cards.

> **I:** "Schools need a health record with immunizations." (Point to the **health record** and **immunizations** cards and point to the **school** card. Motion for the learners to repeat.)
>
> **G:** "Schools need a health record with immunizations."
>
> **I:** "Schools need a health record with a physical exam." (Point to the **health record** and **physical exam** cards and point to the **school** card. Motion for the learners to repeat.)
>
> **G:** "Schools need a health record with a physical exam."

9. Have the group repeat the sentences that correspond to what is needed for school enrollment at least three times.

10. Ask learners to point to the corresponding cards to ensure their comprehension of the terms and the concept.

Comprehension Check

1. Distribute a set of **OK/Not OK** cards to each learner.

2. Hold up various cards and ask learners if the combination of cards is OK or Not OK for school enrollment.

3. Ask the group to hold up the **OK** card if the correct combination that is needed for school enrollment is displayed and the **Not OK** card if the combination contains one or more items that are not needed for school enrollment.
4. Model the comprehension check using the method below.

> **I:** "Health record. Immunizations. Physical exam. OK or Not OK? (Hold up the **OK** and **Not OK** cards and motion for a response.)
>
> **G:** "OK." (Learners should hold up the **OK** card.)
>
> **I:** "Birth certificate. Driver's license. Social Security card. OK or Not OK?" (Hold up the **OK** and **Not OK** cards and motion for a response.)
>
> **G:** "Not OK." (Learners should hold up the **Not OK** card.)

5. Continue with various combinations using the large vocabulary cards from Lessons A and B.
6. Assist learners as necessary.

Oral Language Activity 4

Introduce the Role Play

MATERIALS

Large vocabulary cards (multiple sets of all)

Theme picture

NOTE

Pointing to each word while reading is important to do even if the learners are non-readers or nonliterate.

1. Hold up the theme picture with corresponding noun cards to model the role play.
2. Write the dialogue (see example below) on the board or other visible surface and read it for the group, pointing to each word.

> **Speaker 1:** "What do the children need for school?" (Hold up the **school** card and place it in a visible location. Hold up the **birth certificate** card and motion for a response.)
>
> **Speaker 2:** "They need birth certificates." (Point to the **birth certificate** card.)
>
> **Speaker 1:** "What do the children need for school?" (Hold up the **health record** card and motion for a response.)
>
> **Speaker 2:** "They need health records." (Point to the **health record** card.)
>
> **Speaker 1:** "What do the children need for school?" (Hold up the **physical exam** card and motion for a response.)
>
> **Speaker 2:** "They need physical exam." (Point to the **physical exam** card.)
>
> **Speaker 1:** "What do the children need for school?" (Hold up the **immunizations** card and motion for a response.)
>
> **Speaker 2:** "They need immunizations." (Point to the **immunizations** card.)

3. Perform the dialogue as Speaker 1 and ask the learners to respond as Speaker 2, practicing the entire dialogue at least three times.

Role Play Activity

1. Write the previous dialogue on the board and read it for the group, pointing to each word.
2. Go through the dialogue and have the group respond to the instructor's lines and prompts.
3. Perform the dialogue as a group three times, using the theme picture and realia to dramatize the role play.
4. Assist learners as needed.

> **I:** "What do the children need for school?" (Hold up the **school** card and place it in a visible location. Hold up the **birth certificate** card and motion for a response.)
>
> **G:** "They need birth certificates." (Learners should point to the **birth certificate** card.)
>
> **I:** "What do the children need for school?" (Hold up the **health record** card and motion for a response.)
>
> **G:** "They need health records." (Learners should point to the **health record** card.)
>
> **I:** "What do the children need for school?" (Hold up the **physical exam** card and motion for a response.)
>
> **G:** "They need physical exam." (Learners should point to the **physical exam** card.)
>
> **I:** "What do the children need for school?" (Hold up the **immunizations** card and motion for a response.)
>
> **G:** "They need immunizations." (Learners should point to the **immunizations** card.)

Comprehension Check

1. Shuffle the large vocabulary cards and place them faceup on the table or other available surface.
2. Ask learners the question and use visual prompts and gestures to help learners find the correct corresponding card.

> **I:** "What do the children need for school?" (Hold up the **school** card and place it in a visible location. Hold up the **birth certificate** card. Motion for the group to respond and to find the card on the table or other surface.)
>
> **G:** "They need birth certificates." (Learners should try to pick up the **birth certificate** card.)

3. Ask the learner who picks up the correct card first to repeat the noun or complete sentence.

4. Continue asking the question, using visual prompts, until all of the items for school enrollment are identified.
5. Repeat the process as necessary to ensure the group's comprehension.

Reading Activity

MATERIALS

Large vocabulary cards (from Lessons A & B)

Small word cards

Review

1. Shuffle all of the large target noun cards.
2. Show each card to the group while pronouncing each word slowly and clearly.
3. Run a finger under each word to help learners begin to recognize the words apart from the pictures.
4. Have the learners repeat the nouns at least three times.

> **I:** "Health record." (Point to the term.)
> **G:** "Health record."
> **I:** "Health record." (Underline the term with a finger. Motion for the group to repeat the term.)
> **G:** "Health record."

NOTE

Separating pictures from words should be done gradually and after plenty of practice.

5. Continue to review with the cards, using the pattern above.
6. Fold cards in half to show only the words, to help learners become less dependent on the pictures.
7. Move from group to individual practice as learners become more comfortable reading the words without the assistance of the pictures.

NOTE

The object of the game is to collect all four items needed for school enrollment.

Document Card Activity

1. Display the large vocabulary cards of the items needed for school enrollment for learners to use as a reference **(birth certificate, health record, immunizations,** and **physical exam).**
2. Shuffle the sets of small word cards together and give each player four cards.
3. Put the rest of the cards facedown in a pile in the middle of the group.
4. Have the players take turns drawing a card from the middle pile.
5. Motion for learners to put the card drawn on the bottom of the pile if it is not a card needed to complete the set of four for school enrollment.
6. Allow learners to keep the cards they draw if they discard another card.

7. Model the activity as a group, assisting the learners with reading the words.
8. Continue the activity until one player can show a correct set of four items needed for school enrollment.

Writing Activity

MATERIALS

Large vocabulary cards (from Lessons A & B)

School Checklist activity sheet (one enlarged and one per learner)

Review

1. Shuffle all of the large target noun cards.
2. Show each card to the group while pronouncing each word slowly and clearly.
3. Run a finger under each word to help learners begin to recognize the words apart from the pictures.
4. Have the learners repeat the nouns at least three times.

> **I:** "Health record." (Point to the term.)
> **G:** "Health record."
> **I:** "Health record." (Underline the term with a finger. Motion for the group to repeat the term.)
> **G:** "Health record."

NOTE

Separating pictures from words should be done gradually and after plenty of practice.

5. Continue to review with the cards, using the pattern above.
6. Fold cards in half to show only the words, to help learners become less dependent on the pictures.
7. Move from group to individual practice as learners become more comfortable reading the words without the assistance of the pictures.

School Checklist Activity

1. Distribute a School Checklist activity sheet to each learner.
2. Place an enlarged activity sheet in a visible location to assist the learners.
3. Put the large vocabulary cards from Lessons A and B at the front of the room for learners to use as reference.
4. Ask learners to choose the correct four items required for school enrollment and write them in the spaces provided on their individual activity sheets.
5. Assist learners as necessary. Use the enlarged activity sheet and vocabulary cards to prompt the learners and model how to complete the activity sheet.

Unit Review Activity

MATERIALS

Unit Review activity sheet (one enlarged and one per learner)

Large vocabulary cards (from Lessons A & B)

NOTE

The Unit Review Activity can be done as a group activity for reinforcing the concepts learned in the lesson or done as an individual activity for assessment purposes.

Save and Need for School Activity

1. Use the large vocabulary cards from Lessons A and B to review the vocabulary and concepts from the unit.
2. For review, ask learners if the documents are something to save. Have learners respond Yes or No for each document.
3. Continue the review. Ask learners if the documents are something that is needed for school enrollment. Have learners respond Yes or No for each document.
4. Distribute a copy of the Unit Review activity sheet to each learner. Post an enlarged copy of the activity sheet in the front of the room.
5. Ask learners to complete the activity. If necessary, use the enlarged activity sheet to model checking the documents that they need to save and the documents that they need for school enrollment. Make sure they understand that a document can be checked in both columns.

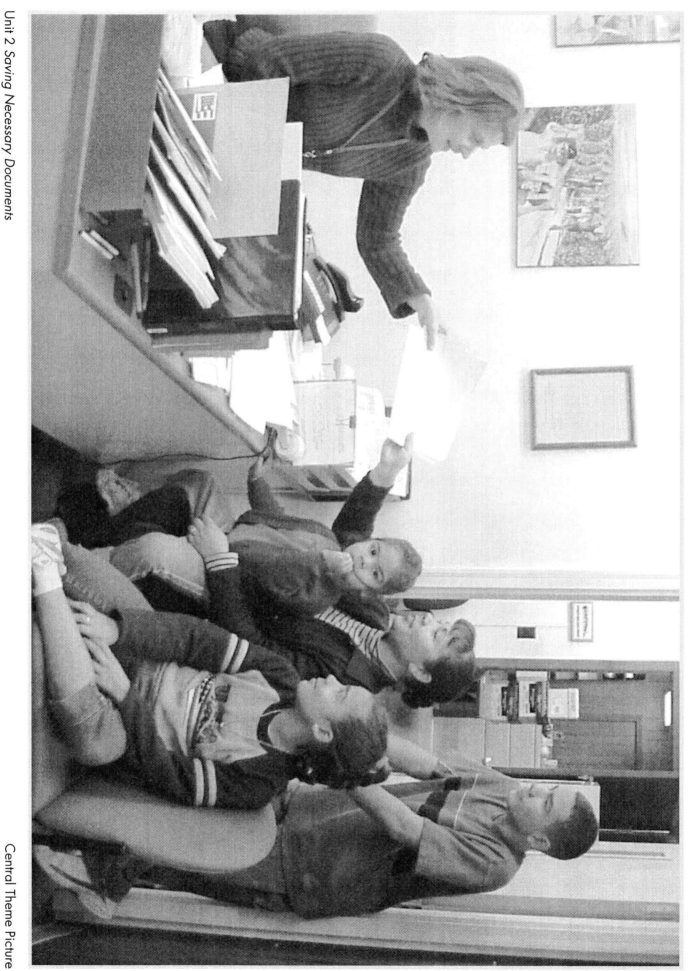

STATE DRIVER'S LICENSE

DRIVER LICENSE

Commissioner of Motor Vehicles
Joe Commissioner

ID: 012 345 678
DOB: **12-15-67**

JUAN CARLOS PADILLA GOMEZ
PO BOX 123
ANYTOWN   NY
12345

SEX: M   EYES: BR   HT: 6-1   CLASS: D

ISSUED: 12-15-05   EXPIRES: 12-15-13

8005456548

Juan Carlos Padilla Gomez

Driver's license

BIRTH CERTIFICATE

Certificate Holders

Name at Birth:
Juan Carlos Padilla Gomez

Date of Birth: 12/15/67   Sex: M X   F

Father's Name: Jose   Padilla   Rodriguez
                  (First, Middle, Last)

Mother's Maiden Name: Augustina Gomez   Garcia
                      (First, Middle, Last)

Adopted: Yes   No X   State of Birth: NY

County of Birth: Anycounty   City of Birth: Anytown

Hospital: Anytown Memorial Hospital

Father's Signature   *Jose Padilla Rodriguez*

Mother's Signature   *Augustina Gomez de Padilla*

Birth certificate

Paid bill

Papers

Social Security card

SOCIAL SECURITY

123 45 6789

THIS NUMBER HAS BEEN ESTABLISHED FOR

Juan Carlos Padilla Gomez

Juan Carlos Padilla Gomez
SIGNATURE

DEPARTMENT OF HEALTH & HUMAN SERVICES · USA

Pay stub

Check Date	Check No.
06/30/05	555

Amount $ 580.01

USA Manufacturing
321 Factory Lane
Anytown, NY 12345

PAY Five hundred eighty dollars and one cent

to the order of JUAN PADILLA GOMEZ
PO BOX 123
ANYTOWN   NY   12345

NON-NEGOTIABLE

USA Manufacturing
321 Factory Lane
Anytown, NY 12345

Employee	Juan Padilla Gomez
Marital Status	Married

Check Date	Check No.
06/30/05	555

Social Security Number	Salary	Federal Exemptions	State Exemptions
123-45-6789	$ 9.50 / hour	2	0

Amount	This Check	Calendar
FEDERAL	88.20	1058.40
FICA	58.14	697.68
MEDICARE	10.28	123.36
STATE	23.37	280.44

This Check	Amount
Gross Pay	760.00
Deductions	179.99
Net Pay	580.01

Birth certificate

Driver's license

Paid bill

Papers

Pay stub

Social Security card

Write the Document Names Activity

Trace the words next to each picture. Write the words on the lines.

Trace Words	Write Words

Birth certificate

Driver's license

Paid bill

Papers

Pay stub

Social Security card

Unit 2 *Saving Necessary Documents* Lesson B *Civic Responsibility*

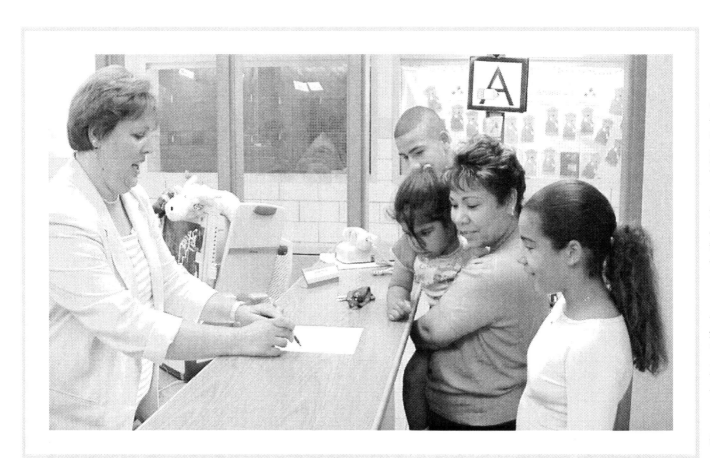

Unit 2 *Saving Necessary Documents* Lesson B *Civic Responsibility*

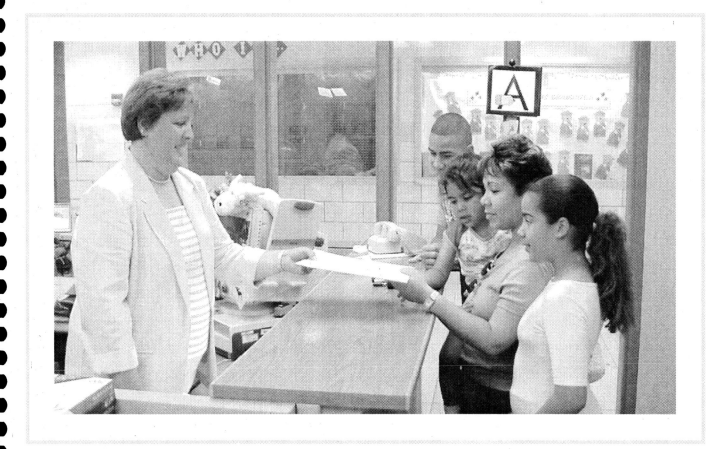

Unit 2 *Saving Necessary Documents* Lesson B *Civic Responsibility*

Storyboard Frame 3

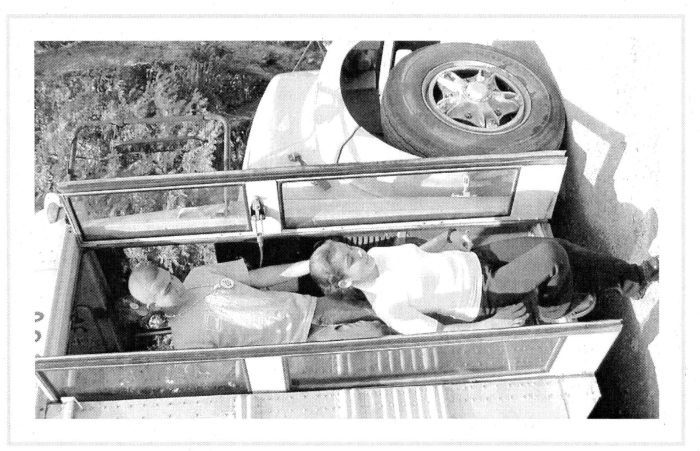

Unit 2 *Saving Necessary Documents* Lesson B *Civic Responsibility*

Storyboard Frame 4 **93**

Children

Health record

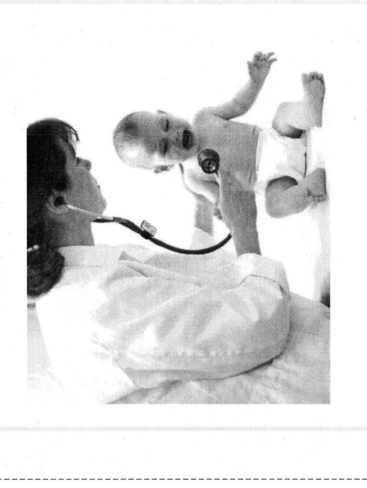

Physical exam

Unit 2 *Saving Necessary Documents: B*

IMMUNIZATION RECORD

AGE ▶ VACCINE ▼	Birth Month	1 Month	2 Months	4 Months	6 Months	12 Months	15 Months	4-6 Years	11-12 Years	14-18 Years
Hepatitis B	Jul 1 1998	Aug 20 1998		Dec 20 1998						
Diphtheria, Tetanus, Pertussis (DTaP)			Oct 1 1998	Dec 15 1998			Sept 3 1999	Sept 5 2002		
Haemophilus influenzae type B (Hib)			Oct 12 1998	Dec 15 1998			Oct 9 1999			
Polio (IPV)			Aug 15 1998	Oct 1 1998		June 8 1999		Sept 5 2002		
Pneumococcal Conjugate (PCV)			Aug 1 1998	Oct 12 1998	Dec 8 1998	June 8 1999				
Measles, Mumps, Rubella			Aug 6 1998			June 1 1999		Sept 5 2002		
Varicella (Chicken pox)						June 1 1999				
Hepatitis A[2]										

Immunizations

Unit 2 *Saving Necessary Documents: B*

School

Yes

No

Children

Health record

School

Physical exam

Immunizations

School Checklist Activity

Look at the pictures and words. Choose the four items needed for school enrollment.
Then make a checklist. Write the four items on the lines.

Checklist for School Enrollment

Health record

☐ _____

Birth certificate

Immunizations

☐ _____

Social Security card

☐ _____

Driver's license

Physical exam

☐ _____

Save and Need for School Activity

Look at the pictures and words. Check the items you need to save.
Check the items you need for school enrollment.

		Save	Need for School Enrollment
1.	Health record	✔	✔
2.	Social Security card		
3.	Birth certificate		
4.	Paid bill		
5.	Immunizations		
6.	Physical exam		
7.	Driver's license		
8.	Pay stub		

Unit 2 *Saving Necessary Documents* Lesson B *Civic Responsibility*   Unit Review Activity

Unit 3

Finding Work

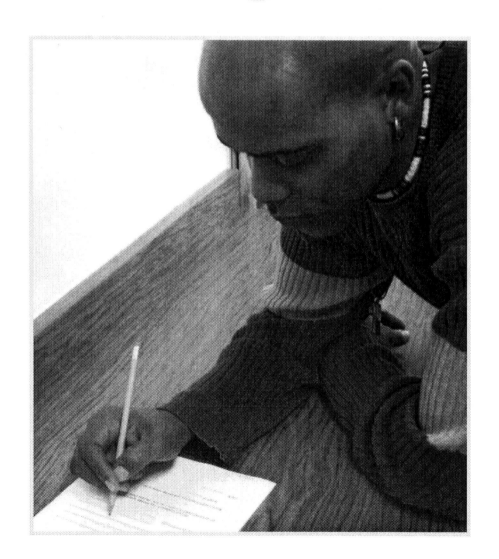

Lesson A - Life Skill

Job Applications

VOCABULARY

NOUNS

Address
Application
Employer
Job
Name
Phone number

VERBS

Save
Write

Objectives

- To enable learners to provide selected information needed to complete a job application
- To help learners understand the importance of keeping personal information available for completing applications

Materials Included

- Central theme picture
- Large reproducible vocabulary cards
- Small word cards (nouns only)
- Application Form cards
- Write or Save activity cards
- Sample Job Application activity sheet
- Complete an Application activity sheet
- **Yes/No** cards

Materials Needed

- Additional instructor copy (enlarged) of the activity sheets and Job Application form
- Pictures (from magazines or books) of houses or apartments and people in various jobs
- Real or toy telephone
- Real or instructor-made job application form
- Manila file folders (one for each learner)
- Pens or pencils (one for each learner)
- Real or instructor-made mock-ups of documents or other important papers

Central Theme Picture

MATERIALS
Theme picture

POSSIBLE RESPONSES
Application

Form

Man

Paper

Pen

Pencil

Social Security card

Table

Write

Introduce Theme Picture

1. Show learners the theme picture and ask for a response.
2. Encourage learners to say anything about the picture that they can.

> **I:** "What's happening in this picture?" (Point out key things about the picture to elicit a response.)

Oral Language Activity 1

MATERIALS

Large noun cards (multiple sets)

Pictures (from magazines or books) of houses or apartments and people in various jobs

A real or toy telephone

Real or instructor-made job application form

Small word cards

Write or Save activity cards

Introduce Target Nouns

1. Show each large noun card to the group, pronouncing each word slowly and clearly.

> **I:** "Name." (Hold up the **name** card and motion for the group to repeat the word.)
> **G:** "Name."
> **I:** "Good. Name." (Hold up the **name** card. Write your first name on the board or on another visible surface. Say your name for the group. Gesture to clarify that it is your name. Then repeat the target noun.)
> **I:** "Name." (Motion for the group to repeat.)
> **G:** "Name."
> **I:** "Name." (Motion for the group to repeat. Put the card at the front of the room.)
> **G:** "Name."

2. Introduce the target nouns (**address, application, employer, job, name,** and **phone number**) using the format above.
3. Use mime, pictures, and realia as necessary to help the group understand the target nouns.
4. Say each word and have the group repeat each one three times.
5. Repeat any words more than three times as necessary.

Concentration

1. Shuffle the Write or Save activity cards (picture cards) with the small word cards.

NOTE

Photocopying the two sets of noun cards onto paper of different colors will help facilitate the matching of pairs. The learner who collects the most pairs wins.

NOTE

A matched pair consists of a picture card and its corresponding word card.

2. Spread cards out on the table facedown so that they are not overlapping.
3. Show learners how to do the activity by turning over two cards.
4. Read or help learners read the cards. Model at least one mismatch (failure) and one match (success).
5. Model getting a matched pair to show how a player with a matched pair is allowed an extra turn.
6. Model getting cards that do not match to show how the cards should be put back facedown on the table.
7. Motion for learners to begin the activity by choosing the first person to start.
8. Have each learner choose two cards and identify them verbally.
9. Assist learners as needed.
10. Motion for learners to hold up the pairs or single cards to show the group as they read them.
11. Count each learner's pairs and single cards (and encourage the group to count along).
12. Have learners read aloud which pairs they collected when the activity is finished.

Comprehension Check

1. Shuffle all of the large noun cards. Use multiple sets if necessary so that each learner gets at least one card.
2. Distribute the cards to the learners at random.
3. Call out each target noun and motion for the learner(s) with the corresponding card to hold it up.
4. Continue calling out target vocabulary and motioning for learners to hold up the corresponding cards.
5. Assist learners as necessary.

Oral Language Activity 2

Introduce Target Verbs

1. Introduce the verbs **save** and **write** through demonstration, pronouncing each word slowly and clearly.
2. Use the large verb cards to reinforce the meaning and associate the verbs with the pictures on the cards.

MATERIALS

Large noun cards

Large verb cards

Small noun cards (excluding **application**)

Manila file folders

Instructor-provided documents or other important papers

Application Form cards (one enlarged and one for each learner)

Yes/No cards

> **I:** "Save." (Show the group that **save** means to keep
> something in a secure place. Place an important paper in a
> manila file folder. Motion for the group to repeat together.)
>
> **G:** "Save."
>
> **I:** "Good. Save." (Hold up the **save** card. Motion for the
> group to repeat.)
>
> **G:** "Save."
>
> **I:** "Save." (Motion for the group to repeat.)
>
> **G:** "Save."

3. Introduce the verb **write** using the format above.
4. Demonstrate the verb **write** by writing on the board, chart paper, or other paper.
5. Say each word and have the group repeat each one three times.
6. Repeat any word more than three times as necessary.

Noun and Verb Combination Activity

1. Use the large vocabulary cards to show the group how to put nouns and the verb **write** together.
2. Model how the nouns and the verb should be paired together for this activity.
3. Help learners understand the terms through mime and with documents and realia.

> **I:** "Write address." (Point to the **address** card. Hold up an
> enlarged Application Form card. Demonstrate writing
> an address on the sample application form. Motion for
> the group to repeat the term.)
>
> **G:** "Write address."
>
> **I:** "Write address." (Point to the **address** card. Hold up the
> **write** card. Motion for the group to repeat the term.)
>
> **G:** "Write address."
>
> **I:** "Write address." (Point to the **address** card. Hold up the
> **write** card. Motion for the group to repeat the term.)
>
> **G:** "Write address."

Noun + Verb Combination Terms

Write name	Write phone number
Write job	Write employer
Write address	

4. Have learners repeat each term at least three times.
5. Help learners make clear distinctions between terms.
6. Distribute Application Form cards (one to each learner).
7. Give learners sets of small noun cards (excluding **application**) to accompany the Application Form cards.

8. Place an enlarged Application Form card in a visible location in the room.

> **I:** "What's this?" (Hold up the **name** card. Motion for a response.)
> **G:** "Name."
> **I:** "What's this?" (Hold up the **address** card. Motion for a response.)
> **G:** "Address."
> **I:** "What's this?" (Hold up the **job** card. Motion for a response.)
> **G:** "Job."
> **I:** "What's this?" (Hold up the **employer** card. Motion for a response.)
> **G:** "Employer."
> **I:** "What's this? (Hold up the **phone number** card. Motion for a response.)
> **G:** "Phone number."

9. Hold up the **name** card and place it on the enlarged Application Form card in the place where a name should be written.
10. Repeat this action and have the learners choose the **name** card from their set of small noun cards to place in the correct place on their individual Application Form cards.

> **I:** "Write name." (Place the **name** card on the Application Form card where name should be written. Hold up the **write** card. Motion for the group to repeat.)
> **G:** "Write name."

11. Using the large vocabulary cards, demonstrate to the group how to fill out the Application Form card. Use the example above to help demonstrate where each card should be placed.
12. Have learners use their small noun cards to fill out their individual Application Form cards.
13. Make sure the group verbalizes each term (**write** + noun) after placing each card in the correct place on the Application Form card.
14. Assist learners as necessary.

Comprehension Check
1. Collect the target noun cards and reshuffle them.
2. Introduce the cards one by one, identifying the nouns correctly and incorrectly at random.
3. Model how to say Yes when the card is correctly identified, and No when it is incorrectly identified. Hold up the appropriate **Yes** or **No** card to reinforce the desired response.

> **I:** "Name." (Hold up the **name** card.)
>
> **I:** "Name. Yes." (Point to the **name** card and nod in agreement. Motion for the learners to repeat.)
>
> **G:** "Yes."
>
> **I:** "Job." (Hold up the **name** card again.)
>
> **I:** "Job. No." (Point to the **name** card and motion disagreement. Motion for the learners to repeat.)
>
> **G:** "No."

4. Continue with other target nouns randomly.
5. Combine **write** through mime with various nouns and use the pattern above to check the group's understanding.
6. Repeat words as necessary.

Oral Language Activity 3

MATERIALS

Large vocabulary cards

Manila file folders (one per learner and one for instructor)

Pens or pencils (one per learner and one for instructor)

Write or Save activity cards (2 sets)

Introduce Saving the Information

1. Place the large**employer** card in a visible location at the front of the room.
2. Hold up the manila folder and the **address** card and place them side by side.

> **I:** "Save address." (Point to the **address** card. Mime saving the address in the manila file folder.)
>
> **G:** "Save address."
>
> **I:** "Save address." (Point to the **address** card. Hold up the **save** card. Motion for the group to repeat.)
>
> **G:** "Save address."
>
> **I:** "Save address." (Point to the **address** card. Hold up the **save** card. Motion for the group to repeat.)
>
> **G:** "Save address."

Noun + Verb Combination Terms

Save address
Save phone number
Save name

3. Have the group repeat each term using the format above.
4. Assist learners as necessary.

Write or Save Activity

1. Distribute a manila file folder and a pen or pencil to each learner so that each has an object to represent **write** and **save.**

2. Have each learner place the **write** and **save** objects in front of him or her.
3. Shuffle two sets of Write or Save activity cards together and place them in a pile facedown in the center of the group.
4. Model how to do the activity.
5. Draw a card from the pile and identify it, using the format below.

> **I:** "Address." (Hold up the **address** card. Point to the manila file folder on it. Show the group that it is the **address** card with a manila file folder symbol next to the picture. Hold up the **save** card to pair with the noun.)
>
> **I:** "Save address." (Hold up a manila file folder. Motion for the group to hold up their own folders and repeat.)
>
> **G:** "Save address."

6. Show the learners a card with a pencil printed on it. Use the **write** card to demonstrate how to pair the noun with the appropriate verb.

> **I:** "Write address." (Hold up the **address** card with the pencil. Point to the pencil. Show the address picture. Hold up the **write** card to pair with the noun. Motion for the group to hold up their own pens or pencils and repeat.)
>
> **G:** "Write address."

7. Continue having each learner draw a card and construct a verb phrase, using the cards, folders, or pencils for assistance.

Comprehension Check

1. Place the **write** card with a pen or pencil and the **save** card with a manila file folder in a visible location in the room.
2. Distribute pens, pencils, manila file folders, and noun cards to learners. Make sure that each learner has at least one noun card.
3. Identify each verb for the group.

> **I:** " Write." (Point to the pen or pencil. Motion for a response.)
>
> **G:** "Write." (Learners should hold up a pen or pencil.)
>
> **I:** "Save." (Point to the manila file folder. Motion for a response.)
>
> **G:** "Save." (Learners should hold up a manila file folder.)

4. Say nouns with a verb. Have learners holding those nouns place them next to the correct verb card and accompanying object.

> **I:** "Save address." (Motion for the learner with the **address** card to place it next to the correct verb card and repeat the phrase.)
>
> **L:** "Save address." (Learner should hold up the **address** card and a manila file folder, then place the **address** card under the instructor's manila file folder).

5. Continuewith other nouns until all of the noun cards have been placed in categories. Make sure that learners hold up the accompanying manila file folder, pen, or pencil to ensure comprehension.

Oral Language Activity 4

MATERIALS

Large vocabulary cards

NOTE

The last learner to hear the term will try to repeat it. The team that retains the phrase correctly will receive a point.

Introduce the Whisper Race Activity

1. Divide the group into two teams.
2. Have each team line up with some distance between the lines.
3. Show the group how to do the activity by whispering a target phrase (**write** or **save** + noun) to a learner.
4. Motion for that learner to whisper the same term to the next learner.

Whisper Race Activity

1. Choose a phrase (**write** or **save** + noun) and whisper it to each group.
2. Have learners whisper the message from one learner to the next down the line.

> **I:** "Write name." (Whisper to both teams. Check that each learner can repeat the phrase.)
>
> **I:** "OK. Go!"
>
> **Speaker 1:** "Write name." (Whispering.)
>
> **Speaker 2:** "Write name." (Whispering.)
>
> **Speaker 3:** "Write name." (Whispering.)
>
> **Speaker 4:** "Write name." (Whispering.)
>
> **Speaker 5:** "Write name."
>
> **I:** "Great work!"

3. Ask the final person in line to repeat the phrase for the group.
4. Give individuals assistance as necessary.
5. Repeat problematic phrases as a group at the end of the activity.

Comprehension Check

1. Hold up two different large vocabulary cards for the group.
2. Identify one of the cards and ask the learners to point to the correct one.

> **I:** "Name." (Hold up a **name** card and an **address** card. Ask the learners to point to the correct card and identify it.)
>
> **G:** "Name." (Learners should point to the **name** card.)

3. Repeatwith other pairs of cards to ensure learners' comprehension.

Reading Activity

Review

1. Shuffle all of the target noun cards.
2. Show each card to the group while pronouncing each word slowly and clearly.
3. Run a finger under each word to help learners begin to recognize the words apart from the pictures.
4. Have the learners repeat the words at least three times.

> **I:** "Employer." (Point to the word. Motion for the group to repeat.)
>
> **G:** "Employer."
>
> **I:** "Employer." (Underline the word with a finger. Motion for the group to repeat.)
>
> **G:** "Employer."

NOTE

Separating words from pictures should be done gradually and after plenty of practice.

5. Continue to review with the cards, using the pattern above.
6. Fold cards in half to show only the words, to help learners become less dependent on the pictures.
7. Move from group to individual practice as learners become more comfortable reading the words without the assistance of the pictures.

Sample Job Application Activity

1. Display the large noun cards (words and pictures) at the front of the room or in another visible location.
2. Post an enlarged Sample Job Application activity sheet at the front of the room.
3. Shuffle the sets of small word cards and place them facedown on a table or other available surface.
4. Model choosing a card from the pile, reading it aloud, and placing it as a label next to the appropriate picture on the enlarged activity sheet.
5. Have the learners take turns choosing cards from the pile and reading them aloud.
6. After each learner reads the card he or she has chosen, ask that the card be placed as a label on the learner's own Sample Job Application activity sheet.

NOTE

If a learner chooses and reads a card that is already on his or her activity sheet, have the learner put the card back on the bottom of the pile and choose another card.

7. Continue until learners have completed their activity sheets.
8. Assist learners as necessary.

Writing Activity

Review

1. Shuffle all of the target noun cards together.
2. Show each card to the group while pronouncing each word slowly and clearly.
3. Run a finger under each word to help learners begin to recognize the words apart from the pictures.
4. Have the learners repeat the words at least three times.

> **I:** "Job." (Point to the word.)
> **G:** "Job."
> **I:** "Job." (Underline the word with a finger. Motion for the group to repeat the word.)
> **G:** "Job."

NOTE

Separating words from pictures should be done gradually and after plenty of practice.

5. Continue to review with the cards, using the pattern above.
6. Fold cards in half to show only the words, to help learners become less dependent on the pictures.
7. Move from group to individual practice as learners become more comfortable reading the words without the assistance of the pictures.

Complete an Application Activity

1. Distribute a copy of the partially completed Complete an Application activity sheet to each learner.
2. If necessary, display the large noun cards (words and pictures) at the front of the room or in another visible location.
3. On the enlarged activity sheet, model for learners how to fill in the missing terms to create a complete job application.
4. Have learners fill in the missing terms on their own activity sheets.
5. Review with learners the personal information already on the activity sheets. Demonstrate how each item of personal information matches the term that learners wrote on the sheet.
6. To complete the activity, assist learners in writing their personal information on the Complete an Application activity sheet. Have them write their own information in the space under the information already present on the activity sheet. Alternatively, prepare copies of blank Complete an Application activity sheets, and have students complete the terms and the personal information.

NOTE

Prior to this activity, help learners practice writing their personal information. You may want to prepare cards with learners' personal information, from which they can copy the information onto the blank activity sheet.

Lesson B – Civic Responsibility

Social Security Cards

VOCABULARY

NOUNS

Employee

Social Security card

Social Security number

VERB

Show

NOTE

Throughout this lesson, make sure that students understand the importance of keeping their Social Security number secure and private. For any group activities, it is best to use replica cards with made-up numbers.

Objectives

- To help learners understand the importance of Social Security cards and numbers
- To ensure that learners know how to use the number and card responsibly

Materials Included

- Large reproducible vocabulary cards
- Bingo boards
- Word Search activity sheet
- Write the Words activity sheet
- **OK/Not OK** cards (page 180)

Materials Needed

- Bingo board markers (paper clips, buttons, dried beans, coins, or other small objects)
- Real or (preferably) instructor-made replicas of Social Security cards
- 3x5 cards with matching and nonmatching Social Security numbers
- Maps
- Photographs or magazine pictures to demonstrate **show**
- Pictures that depict people working
- Real or instructor-made mock-ups of important documents (from Lesson A) or other important papers
- Pen or pencil
- Manila file folder

Civics Introduction

Social Security Cards

The Social Security Act was enacted on August 14, 1935, to create a national social insurance system for the benefit of retired or disabled persons or surviving relatives of deceased workers. Citizens and Legal Permanent Residents (LPRs) have unique membership numbers in this system, called Social Security numbers (SSNs). These numbers, 9 digits long (in a 3-2-4 number sequence), are printed on Social Security cards and are used for filing taxes every year. Social Security benefits are based on income over the recipient's lifetime; thus income filed using a SSN allows the government to develop an employment and earnings history for a specific individual.

When applying for a new job, an employer must see a valid Social Security card to establish a worker's earnings history, which will include declared earnings and withholdings and will allow for the filing of a W-4 form for the employee. From this point, both the employer and the employee begin contributing into the Social Security system. It is important for employees to always use their own Social Security numbers (SSNs) to assure proper earning credit. Filing income tax also requires the use of an SSN.

Social Security cards are also used for identification purposes. There are three types of Social Security cards available for anyone who is lawfully admitted to the U.S. The first type is only available for citizens and Legal Permanent Residents (LPRs). The second is available for people who have legally entered the U.S. but do not have work authorization from the Department of Homeland Security, or DHS (such as those possessing student visas), and bears the words NOT VALID FOR EMPLOYMENT. The last type is for people who have DHS authorization to work temporarily in the U.S. These cards bear the words VALID FOR WORK ONLY WITH DHS AUTHORIZATION (or, for cards issued prior to April, 2004, WITH INS AUTHORIZATION).

New arrivals may not be aware of the compelling importance of Social Security cards and the consequences of their misuse. Furthermore, some individuals with compromised legal status may have acquired erroneous information regarding the use of Social Security cards and numbers. Illegal behaviors include not filing taxes with the correct Social Security number, selling or buying Social Security numbers, or creating false numbers. Anyone using a false SSN is committing Social Security fraud or ID theft, both of which are federal offenses that can result in deportation, denial of readmittance into the U.S., or denial of ability to legally enter the U.S. For these reasons it is important that newly arrived, non-English-speaking adults learn about their responsibilities as Social Security card holders.

http://www.ssa.gov/kids/history.htm (viewed 9/14/05)
http://www.ssa.gov/immigration/documents.htm (viewed 9/14/05)

Oral Language Activity 1

MATERIALS

Large noun cards (from Lessons A & B)

Bingo boards and markers

Local maps

Pictures showing people working

Real or, (preferably) instructor-made replicas of Social Security cards

Introduce Target Nouns

1. Hold up each noun card and pronounce each word slowly and clearly.
2. Motion for learners to repeat each word.
3. Use pictures, realia, and mime as necessary to connect each noun with the learners' prior knowledge.

> **I:** "Social Security card." (Hold up the card for **Social Security card**. Motion for the group to repeat.)
>
> **G:** "Social Security card."
>
> **I:** "Social Security card." (Hold up a replica social security card and motion for the group to repeat.)
>
> **G:** "Social Security card."
>
> **I:** "Social Security card." (Hold up the card for **Social Security card** and the replica card. Motion for the group to repeat.)
>
> **G:** "Social Security card."

4. Use the vocabulary cards in combination with pictures of people working and replica Social Security cards to introduce the other target nouns.

Suggested Realia

Employee—use local maps to illustrate work locations that learners may be familiar with; use magazine pictures of people working

Social Security number—use small objects (buttons, paper clips, coins of the same value, etc.) to count and practice various numbers (1-10); use the replica Social Security cards to refer to the specific number

5. Have learners repeat each word at least three times.
6. Repeat pronunciation and practice the words more than three times as necessary.

Picture Bingo Activity

1. Distribute one bingo board to each learner.
2. Use the large noun cards from Lessons A and B to prompt the learners. Use cards matching the pictures on the bingo boards (see list on next page).

Pictures on Bingo Boards

Address	Name
Application	Phone number
Employee	Social Security card
Employer	Social Security number
Job	

3. Shuffle or mix together the large noun cards. Put the cards in an envelope or basket.
4. Model the game for learners. Draw a card. Show the card to the group and identify it verbally.
5. Have learners mark their boards on the square corresponding to the noun card drawn, using scraps of paper or small objects.
6. Have a learner draw a card and hold it up. Ask the group to identify the vocabulary term pictured.
7. Continue the game by asking each learner to draw a card and have the entire group say each vocabulary word drawn. If necessary, prompt learners by saying the word and having the group repeat.
8. Once a learner has gotten Bingo, rotate the bingo boards, reshuffle the cards, and do the activity again for additional practice.

Comprehension Check

1. Hold up two noun cards and identify one correctly.
2. Have the group repeat the noun and point to the card that was identified.
3. Continue with other pairs of noun cards.

> **I:** "Social Security card." (Hold up the **Social Security card** and **employee** cards. Motion for a response.)
>
> **G:** "Social Security card." (Learners should point to the card for **Social Security card**.)

NOTE

Three marked boxes in a row (horizontally, vertically, or diagonally) = Bingo.

Oral Language Activity 2

MATERIALS

Large noun card for **Social Security card** (from Lesson B)

Large noun card for **application** (from Lesson A), enlarged if necessary to see information clearly

Instructor-made replica Social Security cards or copies from the large noun card, each with a different number

3x5 cards with matching and nonmatching examples of Social Security numbers (one per card)

OK/Not OK cards (one set per learner)

Introduce the No-Match Concept

1. Hold up the large noun card for **Social Security card.** Have the group identify it, and use it to review other target words.

> **I:** "What's this?" (Hold up the large noun card for **Social Security card.** Motion for a response.)
>
> **G:** "Social Security card."
>
> **I:** "Good. What's this?" (Point to the name on the card. Motion for a response.)
>
> **G:** "Name."
>
> **I:** "Good. What's this?" (Point to the number on the card. Motion for a response.)
>
> **G:** "Social Security number."
>
> **I:** "Great."

2. Write several different Social Security numbers (see suggestions below) on the board or other visible surface. Write some matching and some nonmatching pairs.
3. Show the learners which numbers match (OK) and which numbers do not match (Not OK).
4. Distribute sets of **OK/Not OK** cards to each learner.
5. Practice the concept by pointing to pairs of numbers, matching and nonmatching, and asking learners to hold up the appropriate **OK** or **Not OK** card.
6. Demonstrate the concept of no-match (Not OK) on documents. Use the large noun card for **Social Security card** and a copy of the **application** card (from Lesson A), enlarged if necessary. On the application, write a Social Security number that does not match the number on the card for **Social Security card.**

Suggested Social Security Numbers

111-22-3456	111-22-3456
121-21-2121	131-30-3131
999-88-77777	999-85-7771
555-44-3333	555-44-3333

OK or Not OK?

1. Distribute sets of **OK/Not OK** cards to each learner.
2. Show the group pairs of 3x5 cards with both matching and nonmatching sample Social Security numbers.
3. Ask the group to decide if the pair of cards is OK or Not OK.
4. Have learners hold up the **OK** card if the numbers in the pair match. Have them hold up the **Not OK** card if the numbers do not match.

5. Assist learners as necessary to ensure understanding of the concept.
6. For additional practice, show the group pairs of replica Social Security cards and job applications with both matching and nonmatching Social Security numbers.

Comprehension Check

1. Write pairs of matching and nonmatching Social Security numbers on the board or other visible surface.
2. Distribute sets of **OK/Not OK** cards to each learner.
3. Ask the group to decide if the pairs of numbers are OK or Not OK.
4. Repeat with enough matching and nonmatching sets to ensure learner comprehension.

> **I:** "OK?" (Point to a pair of matching numbers and motion for a response.)
> **G:** "OK." (Learners should hold up the **OK** card.)
> **I:** "OK?" (Point to a pair of nonmatching numbers and motion for a response.)
> **G:** "Not OK." (Learners should hold up the **Not OK** card.)

Oral Language Activity 3

Introduce the Verb

MATERIALS

Large noun cards (from Lessons A & B)

Large verb cards (from Lesson A)

A manila file folder

A pen or pencil

Real or instructor-made mock-ups of important documents (from Lesson A) or other important papers

1. Demonstrate the verb **show,** pronouncing the word slowly and clearly.
2. Motion for learners to repeat the term at least three times.

> **I:** "Show." (Show a family photo or other object to the group, emphasizing the action. Motion for the group to repeat.)
> **G:** "Show."
> **I:** "Show." (Repeat the word with the action and motion for the group to repeat the term.)
> **G:** "Show."
> **I:** "Show." (Motion for the group to repeat.)
> **G:** "Show."

3. Demonstrate the verb with various photos or objects, to ensure that learners associate the verb **show** with the action, not the object being shown.
4. Review verbs **write** and **save** through demonstration. Use the verb cards from Lesson A to reinforce the concepts.

5. Have learners repeat each term at least three times.
6. Repeat and practice the words more than three times as necessary.

NOTE

The purpose of this activity is to help learners understand what to do with a Social Security card and Social Security number when applying for a job.

Social Security Card for Employment Activity

1. Introduce the group to a scenario faced by potential employees looking for work.
2. Have the learners repeat the scenario for comprehension and understanding of the concept.
3. Use vocabulary cards to prompt learners to practice the scenario verbally.

Order of Scenario

1. Show Social Security number to employer.
2. Save Social Security card.
3. Write application.

I: "Show Social Security number to employer." (Hold up the **Social Security** and **employer** cards and motion for the learners to repeat.)

G: "Show Social Security number to employer."

I: "Save Social Security card." (Hold up the card for **Social Security card** and place it in a manila file folder. Motion for the learners to repeat.)

G: "Save Social Security card."

I: "Write application." (Hold up the **application** card and a pen or pencil. Motion for the group to repeat.)

G: "Write application."

4. For additional practice, prompt individual learners to repeat the scenario.

NOTE

Multiple sets of the vocabulary cards may be needed for this activity.

Comprehension Check

1. Shuffle the cards used for this activity (**employer, Social Security number, Social Security card,** and **application).**
2. Distribute the cards to the learners so that each learner has at least one card.
3. Call out each phrase of the scenario and motion for the learner(s) with the corresponding card to hold it up after the phrase has been said.

1. Show Social Security number to employer.
2. Save Social Security card.
3. Write application.

4. Continue calling out phrases. With each one, motion for learners to hold up the corresponding cards.
5. Assist learners as necessary.

Oral Language Activity 4

Introduce the Dialogue

1. Write the sample dialogue (see example below) on the board or on chart paper.
2. Read through each line slowly and clearly.
3. Perform the dialogue as Speaker 1, having the learners respond as Speaker 2.

MATERIALS

Large noun cards (from Lessons A & B)

OK/Not OK cards (one set for each learner)

Speaker 1: "What do you need to do?" (Hold up the **Social Security number** and **employer** cards. Motion for the group to respond.)

Speaker 2: "Show Social Security number to employer."

Speaker 1: "What do you need to do?" (Hold up the card for **Social Security card.** Place the card in a manila file folder. Motion for the group to respond.)

Speaker 2: "Save Social Security card."

Speaker 1: "What do you need to do?" (Hold up the **application** card and demonstrate writing the application. Motion for the group to respond.)

Speaker 2: "Write application."

4. Repeat the dialogue at least three times.

Dialogue Activity

1. Present the dialogue to the group, reading through each line slowly and clearly.
2. Use the large noun cards to prompt the correct responses.
3. Point to each word in the dialogue while reading.
4. Perform the dialogue as Speaker 1, having learners respond as Speaker 2.

NOTE

Pointing to the words while reading is important to do even if the learners are non-readers or nonliterate.

> **Speaker 1:** "What do you need to do?" (Hold up the **Social Security number** and **employer** cards. Point to the number on the Social Security card. Motion for the group to respond.)
>
> **Speaker 2:** "Show Social Security number to employer."
>
> **Speaker 1:** "What do you need to do?" (Hold up the card for **Social Security card.** Place the card in a manila file folder. Motion for the group to respond.)
>
> **Speaker 2:** "Save Social Security card."
>
> **Speaker 1:** "What do you need to do?" (Hold up the **application** card and demonstrate writing the application. Motion for the group to respond.)
>
> **Speaker 2:** "Write application."

5. Ask each question using the verbal and visual prompts, and motion for the group to respond.
6. Make sure that the dialogue is practiced as a group at least three times.
7. Distribute sets of the noun cards among the learners. Have learners review the dialogue in pairs or small groups. In each pair or small group, have one learner hold up the appropriate cards and ask the questions. Have the other learner or learners respond to the verbal prompts.
8. Assist learners as necessary.

Comprehension Check

1. Distribute sets of **OK/Not OK** cards to learners.
2. Hold up the cards that represent each line of the dialogue. Say the line that is represented by the cards or a different line at random.
3. Ask the group to decide if the dialogue line matches the situation displayed in the cards. Ask them if the match is OK or Not OK.

> **I:** "Show Social Security number to employer." (Hold up the **Social Security number** and **employer** cards. Motion for a response.)
>
> **G:** "OK." (Learners should hold up the **OK** card.)
>
> **I:** "Show Social Security number to employer." (Hold up the **application** and **employer** cards. Motion for a response.)
>
> **G:** "Not OK." (Learners should hold up the **Not OK** card.)

4. Assist learners as necessary.

Reading Activity

MATERIALS

Large noun and verb cards

Word Search activity sheet (one enlarged and one per learner)

Review

1. Shuffle the large noun and verb cards.
2. Show each card to the group while pronouncing each word slowly and clearly.
3. Run a finger under each word to help learners begin to recognize the words apart from the pictures.
4. Have the learners repeat the words at least three times.

> **I:** "Employee." (Point to the word. Motion for learners to repeat.)
>
> **G:** "Employee."
>
> **I:** "Employee." (Underline the word with a finger. Motion for the group to repeat the word.)
>
> **G:** "Employee."

NOTE

Separating words from pictures should be done gradually and after plenty of practice.

5. Continue to review with the cards, using the pattern above.
6. Fold cards in half to show only the words, to help learners become less dependent on the pictures.
7. Move from group to individual practice as learners become more comfortable reading the words without the assistance of the pictures.

Word Search Activity

1. Pass out a Word Search activity sheet to each learner.
2. Post the enlarged Word Search activity sheet in the front of the room.
3. Using the enlarged version, show learners how to use the pictures and words listed at the top to locate words in the word search.
4. Choose a word from the list to locate in the word search.
5. Read the word for the learners and point to the picture that represents it.
6. Demonstrate how to look in the Word Search for the word written under the picture.
7. Model finding the word, pointing to each letter in the word. Then demonstrate on the enlarged sheet how to circle the word that is found.
8. Have the learners say each word from the list before they begin their search. Have them complete their own Word Search activity sheets.
9. Assist learners as necessary.

Writing Activity

MATERIALS

Large noun cards

Write the Words activity sheet (one enlarged and one per learner)

OK/Not OK cards

NOTE

Separating words from pictures should be done gradually and after plenty of practice.

Review

1. Shuffle the large noun cards.
2. Show each card to the group while pronouncing each word slowly and clearly.
3. Run a finger under each word to help learners begin to recognize the words apart from the pictures.
4. Have the learners repeat the words at least three times.

> **I:** "Social Security number." (Point to the word.)
> **G:** "Social Security number."
> **I:** "Social Security number." (Underline the word with a finger. Motion for the group to repeat the word.)
> **G:** "Social Security number."

5. Continue to review with the cards, using the pattern above.
6. Fold cards in half to show only the words, to help learners become less dependent on the pictures.
7. Move from group to individual practice as learners become more comfortable reading the words without the assistance of the pictures.

Write the Words Activity

1. Place the large noun cards as well as an enlarged version of the activity sheet on the board or in another visible location.
2. Pass out a Write the Words activity sheet to each learner.
3. Demonstrate how the group can use the posted cards to help them fill in the missing information on the activity sheet.
4. Assist learners as necessary.
5. If necessary, give learners copies of the activity sheet with the words already filled in. Have them trace the words.

Unit Review Activity

MATERIALS

Unit Review activity sheet (one enlarged and one per learner)

Large vocabulary cards (from Lesson A)

Large vocabulary card for **Social Security number**

NOTE

The Unit Review Activity can be done as a group activity for reinforcing the concepts learned in the lesson or done as an individual activity for assessment purposes.

Match Activities

1. Use the large vocabulary cards from LessonA and the **Social Security number** card to review the vocabulary and concepts from the unit.
2. Distribute a copy of the Unit Review activity sheet to each learner. Post an enlarged copy of the activity sheet in the front of the room.
3. Using the enlarged activity sheet, model how to complete the first activity. Read the Social Security number on the first Social Security card. Read each of the Social Security numbers on the application forms until a match is found. Demonstrate how to draw a line from the Social Security card to the application form with the matching number.
4. On the enlarged activity sheet, use the example item (picture of **address** and space for address on the application form) to model how to match the pictures and the appropriate spaces on the form. If necessary, point to each item written on the application form and prompt learners to identify what kind of item it is.
5. Ask learners to complete the activities. If necessary, use the enlarged activity sheet to give learners further models or assistance.

Central Theme Picture

Application

Unit 3 *Finding Work* Lesson A *Life Skill*

Address

123 Main Street
Anytown, NY 12345

Unit 3 *Finding Work* Lesson A *Life Skill*

Employer

✂ -

Job

Phone number

Unit 3 *Finding Work* Lesson A *Life Skill*

Name

Large Vocabulary Cards

Unit 3 *Finding Work* Lesson A *Life Skill*

Save

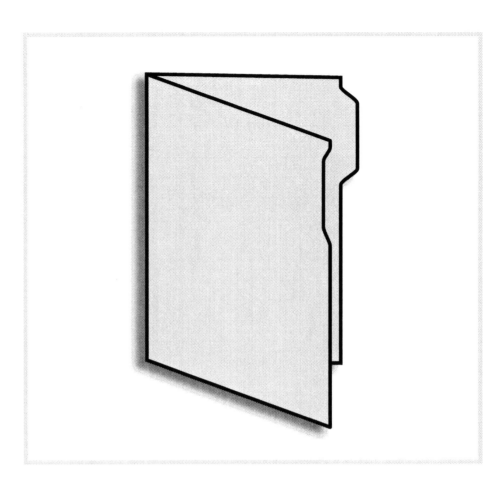

✂ -

Write

Address

Application

Employer

Job

Name

Phone number

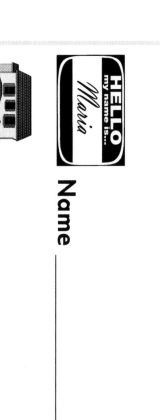

HELLO my name is... Maria

Name _____

123 Main Street
Anytown, NY 12345

Address _____

Job _____

Employer _____

Phone number _____

234-5678
987-654...

✂ -

HELLO my name is... Maria

Name _____

123 Main Street
Anytown, NY 12345

Address _____

Job _____

Employer _____

Phone number _____

234-5678
987-654...

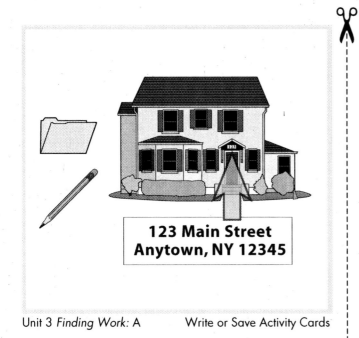

Unit 3 *Finding Work:* A   Write or Save Activity Cards

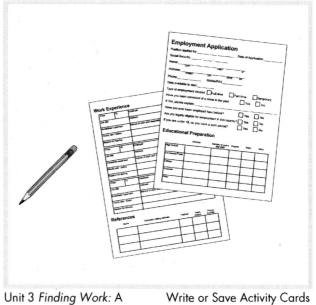

Unit 3 *Finding Work:* A   Write or Save Activity Cards

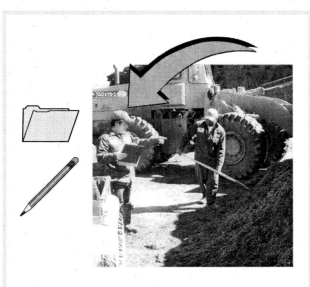

Unit 3 *Finding Work:* A   Write or Save Activity Cards

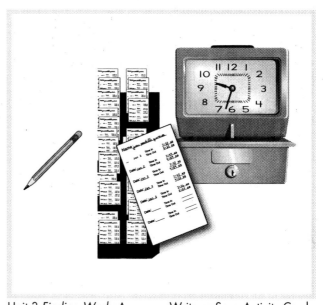

Unit 3 *Finding Work:* A   Write or Save Activity Cards

Unit 3 *Finding Work:* A   Write or Save Activity Cards

Unit 3 *Finding Work:* A   Write or Save Activity Cards

131

Sample Job Application Activity

Use the small noun cards to label the sample job application.

Sample Application

_____   _____

123 Main Street
Anytown, NY 12345

_____   _____

_____

Complete an Application Activity

Fill in the missing terms. Create a job application.

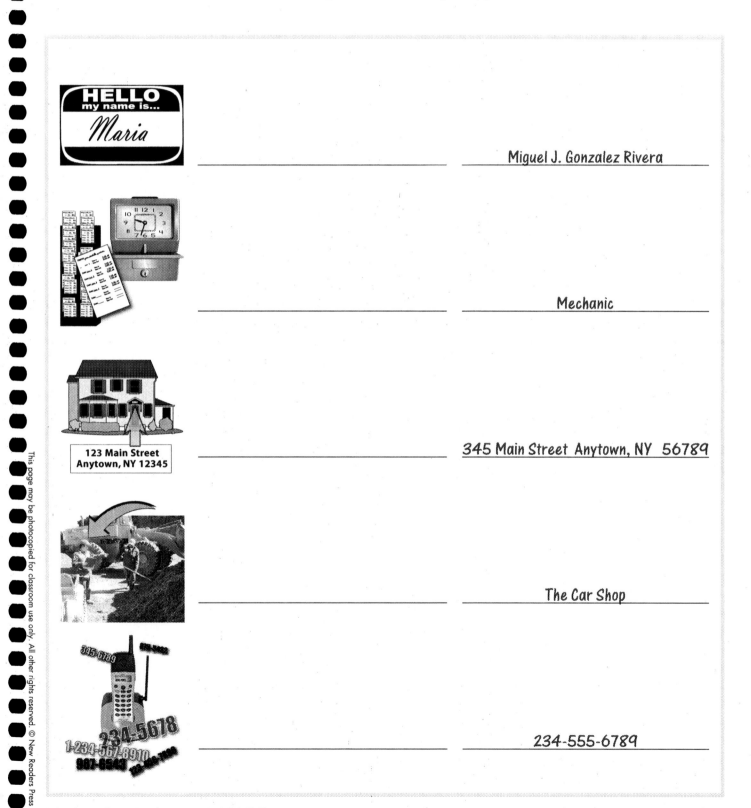

Miguel J. Gonzalez Rivera

Mechanic

345 Main Street Anytown, NY 56789

The Car Shop

234-555-6789

Employee

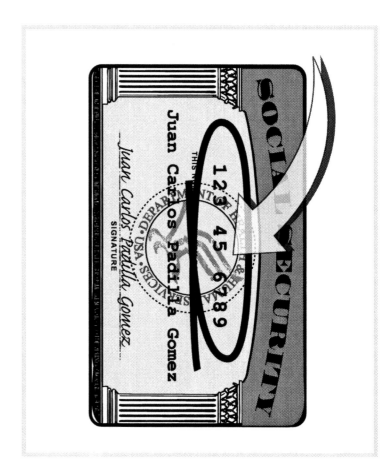

Social Security number

Yes

No

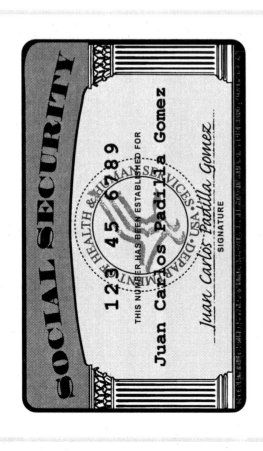

Social Security card

Mini Picture Bingo　　　Board 1

Mini Picture Bingo　　　Board 2

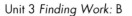

Mini Picture Bingo　　　Board 3

Mini Picture Bingo　　　Board 4

Word Search Activity

Look at the pictures and words. Find the three terms (horizontally, diagonally, or vertically) in the word search. Circle them.

Employee

Social Security number

Social Security card

s	i	m	c	n	t	q	z	f	g	h	e	n	k	n	d	o	m	h	o
o	o	k	s	y	n	u	b	t	s	f	g	e	n	b	s	t	l	k	l
g	y	c	u	e	s	j	l	e	t	q	n	m	h	i	p	w	s	h	d
p	u	x	i	n	y	f	a	l	k	p	n	p	a	d	o	z	t	p	u
g	n	u	y	a	p	z	d	t	s	t	d	l	m	c	x	f	n	g	t
f	h	j	k	p	l	k	n	n	l	h	u	o	n	t	l	y	o	p	y
f	z	e	s	d	x	s	l	m	d	b	i	y	w	l	a	g	u	q	c
o	y	o	l	l	m	c	e	b	m	c	j	e	o	t	a	m	o	u	n
l	t	o	c	d	q	s	s	c	q	s	a	e	o	n	t	h	e	n	k
m	f	i	u	r	n	u	m	c	u	u	l	a	f	h	j	k	e	s	m
f	k	d	u	a	d	h	q	s	a	r	r	w	s	t	a	u	a	y	g
t	p	b	j	k	s	x	m	r	n	i	i	p	u	a	n	i	f	f	x
s	l	y	o	p	f	h	j	k	e	c	l	t	m	s	x	z	h	y	c
s	o	c	i	a	l	s	e	c	u	r	i	t	y	n	u	m	b	e	r
s	h	n	i	r	h	b	a	b	g	u	n	d	o	c	f	h	j	k	r
j	l	e	x	f	h	d	i	g	h	e	n	u	e	j	a	t	u	d	o
u	f	e	o	f	t	u	d	o	f	u	k	m	e	a	c	r	r	m	a
p	k	x	z	s	t	y	b	e	s	j	l	e	s	t	p	x	d	o	n

Write the Words Activity

Look at each picture. Write the correct words on the lines.

_____ _____ _____

_____ _____ _____

Matching Activities

Look at each Social Security card. Find the matching number on an application. Draw a line between the matching documents.

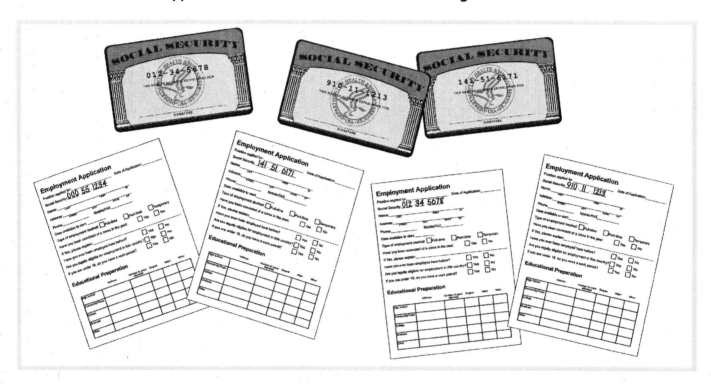

Label the parts of the application. Draw a line from each picture to the correct space on the application.

Unit 4

Preparing for Tax Time

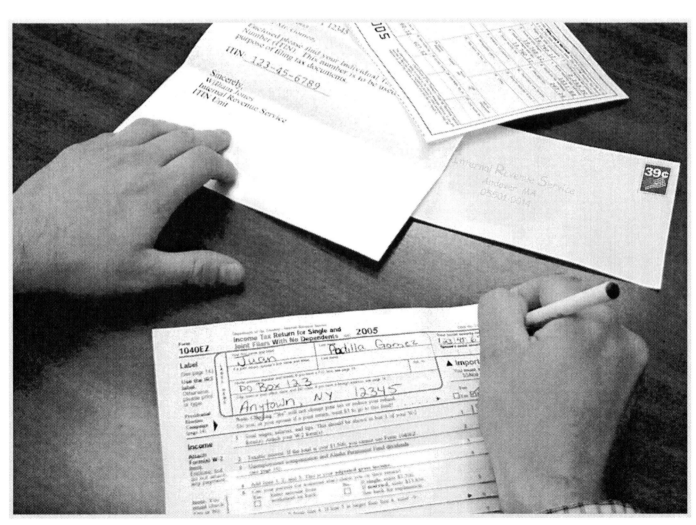

Lesson A - Life Skill

Pay Stubs & Work Documents

VOCABULARY

NOUNS

Money

Pay stub

Tax

W-2

ADJECTIVE

Important

VERBS

Copy

Save

QUESTION

How much is it?

Objectives

- To give learners an understanding of basic work documents
- To make sure learners understand the importance of saving documents for tax purposes

Materials Included

- Central theme picture
- Large reproducible vocabulary cards
- Comprehension Check activity sheet
- Document Matching activity sheet
- Checklist activity sheet
- **Yes/No** cards
- **OK/Not OK** cards (page 180)

Materials Needed

- Manila file folders or large envelopes
- Additional instructor copy (enlarged) of the activity sheets
- Real or instructor-made replicas of pay stubs, W-2s, and tax forms
- Restaurant and/or store receipts
- Real or play money, including coins
- A wallet or a purse
- Instructor-made price cards showing varying amounts
- Picture of a photocopying machine (e.g., from a catalog or magazine)

Central Theme Picture

Introduce Theme Picture

1. Show learners the theme picture and ask for a response.
2. Encourage learners to say anything about the picture that they can.

> **I:** "What's happening in this picture?" (Point out key things about the picture to elicit a response.)

Oral Language Activity 1

Introduce Target Nouns

1. Introduce new vocabulary terms **(money, pay stub,** and **W-2)** to the group.
2. Use realia as necessary to give the learners a solid understanding of new vocabulary terms.
3. Introduce **money** by holding up real or play paper money and distributing bills to each learner while saying the word.

> **I:** "Money." (Hold up the **money** card and real or play money. Pass out a bill to each learner. Motion for the group to repeat together.)
>
> **G:** "Money."
>
> **I:** "Good. Money." (Motion for the group to repeat the word and hold up their bills.)
>
> **G:** "Money." (Learners should hold up their bills.)
>
> **I:** "Money." (Motion for the group to repeat. Put the card at the front of the room.)
>
> **G:** "Money."

4. Repeat introducing the concept of **money** by using real or play coins. Follow the format above. Put the **money** card at the front of the room after learners have repeated the word at least three times.
5. Introduce the remaining nouns **(pay stub** and **W-2)** using the method above.
6. Use multiple copies of pay stubs and W-2s. Distribute them to learners to help them associate the word with an actual document.

7. Say each word and have the group repeat each one three times. Follow the previous format, using the appropriate documents in place of the bills or coins.
8. Repeat any words more than three times as necessary.
9. Collect all the money and documents before continuing on to the activity.

Match the Cards to Realia Activity

1. Mix all of the documents and real or play money together, and place them in a pile on the table or other visible surface.
2. Distribute the items to the group, passing out documents and money piece by piece until all of the materials are distributed.
3. Shuffle the corresponding noun cards **(money, pay stub,** and **W-2)** and hold up each card one at a time.
4. Ask the learners to repeat each word and hold up the corresponding materials.

> **I:** "Money." (Motion for the learners to find an example of money from their pile and hold it up. Ask the learners to repeat the word.)
> **G:** "Money." (Learners should hold up money.)
> **I:** "W-2." (Motion for the learners to find examples of W-2s from their pile and hold them up. Ask the learners to repeat the word.)
> **G:** "W-2." (Learners should hold up W-2s.)
> **I:** "Pay stub." (Motion for the learners to find examples of pay stubs from their pile and hold them up. Ask the learners to repeat the word.)
> **G:** "Pay stub." (Learners should hold up pay stubs.)

5. Repeat several times, varying the order of the vocabulary cards presented.

Comprehension Check

1. Hold up two different types of documents for the group.
2. Identify one of the documents and ask the learners to point to the correct one.

> **I:** "Pay stub." (Hold up a W-2 and a pay stub. Ask the learners to point to the correct material and identify it by name.)
> **G:** "Pay stub." (Learners should point to the pay stub.)

3. Repeat the check with varying pairs to ensure learners' understanding of the new vocabulary.

Oral Language Activity 2

MATERIALS

Large question card

Large noun cards

Instructor-made price cards

Restaurant or store receipts

Yes/No cards

NOTE

Learners will need to have an understanding of U.S. currency and numbers for this activity.

Introduce Question

1. Holdup the question card and point to the shopper in the picture.
2. Pronounce each word in the question slowly and clearly.
3. Introduce the question in two parts.Ask learners to repeat each word of the question. Then present the whole question and have learners repeat.

> **I:** "How much is it?" (Point to the shopper in the picture and the item that the shopper wishes to purchase.)
>
> **I:** "How much is it?" (Point to the picture.)
>
> **I:** "How much . . . " (Motion for the learners to repeat.)
>
> **G:** "How much . . . "
>
> **I:** "How much . . . " (Motion for the learners to repeat.)
>
> **G:** "How much . . . "
>
> **I:** ". . . is it?" (Motion for the learners to repeat.)
>
> **G:** ". . . is it?"
>
> **I:** ". . . is it?" (Motion for the learners to repeat.)
>
> **G:** ". . . is it?"
>
> **I:** "How much is it?" (Point to the shopper in the picture and the item that the shopper wishes to purchase. Motion for the group to repeat.)
>
> **G:** "How much is it?"

4. Have learners repeat the question at least three times.
5. Hold up cards with various prices written in numeric form for the learners to identify.
6. Review numbers and monetary amounts as necessary to help learners respond to the question *How much is it?*

> **I:** "How much is it?" (Hold up an instructor-made price card and motion for a response.)
>
> **G:** "One dollar."

7. Model the pronunciation of the price and have learners repeat as necessary to help learners say the price accurately.
8. Continue with various prices that use different combinations of numbers and also use various combinations of ones, tens, and hundreds.

Example Prices

$1.00	$18.99	$.37
$5.84	$753.01	$205.00

Looking for Amounts Activity

1. Review all of the target nouns introduced in Oral Language Activity 1.
2. Introduce the noun **tax** using a pay stub to illustrate the concept.

> **I:** "Tax." (Hold up the **tax** card. Point to the place on the pay stub where federal or state tax is shown.)
>
> **I:** "Tax." (Motion for the group to repeat.)
>
> **G:** "Tax."
>
> **I:** "Tax." (Motion for the group to repeat.)
>
> **G:** "Tax."
>
> **I:** "Tax." (Motion for the group to repeat.)
>
> **G:** "Tax."

3. Reinforce the meaning of **tax** by showing sales receipts from stores or restaurants to help the group understand the concept.
4. Make sure the group has a solid understanding of all of the target nouns and the question *How much is it?* before continuing with the activity.
5. Use the **W-2** and **pay stub** cards to help learners practice identifying tax amounts.

> **I:** "What's this?" (Point to the federal tax line on the **W-2** card. Motion for a response.)
>
> **G:** "Tax."
>
> **I:** "How much is it?" (Write a dollar sign and question mark on the board or on chart paper. Motion for the group to respond.)
>
> **G:** "$2,293.20."
>
> **I:** "Great! What's this?" (Hold up the **pay stub** card and motion for a response.)
>
> **G:** "Pay stub."
>
> **I:** "OK. How much is it?" (Point to the net pay amount and motion for a response.)
>
> **G:** "$580.01."
>
> **I:** "Good work."

6. Use the format above to ask the group about tax amounts on other documents and sales receipts.
7. Assist learners as necessary.

Comprehension Check

1. Hold up one of the vocabulary cards **(pay stub, money, W-2, or tax).**
2. Associate a dollar amount with each card.

Examples

pay stub – $175.00	money – $306.00
W-2 – $4,200.00	tax – $840.00

3. Ask learners to listen and decide if the amount written on the card matches the one said by the instructor.

> **I:** "$1,700.00." (Hold up pay stub marked with $175.00. Motion for a response.)
>
> **I:** "Yes or No?" (Hold up the **Yes** and **No** cards. Motion for a response.)
>
> **G:** "No."
>
> **I:** "$306.00." (Hold up money worth $306.00. Motion for a response.)
>
> **I:** "Yes or No?" (Hold up the **Yes** and **No** cards. Motion for a response.)
>
> **G:** "Yes."

4. Identify correct and incorrect amounts of money at random.
5. Have learners decide if the amount said matches the amount written on each document.

Oral Language Activity 3

MATERIALS

Manila file folder(s) and/or envelopes

W-2s, pay stubs, and receipts

Real or play money (bills and coins)

A wallet or a purse

A picture of a photocopying machine

Yes/No cards

Comprehension Check activity sheet (one for each learner)

Introduce the Adjective and Verbs

1. Introduce each verb and adjective slowly and clearly. Use pictures, mime, and realia to teach the meaning of each term.

> **I:** "Copy." (Hold up the picture of a photocopying machine. Hold up an important document and some coins. Motion for the learners to repeat.)
>
> **G:** "Copy."
>
> **I:** "Copy." (Mime making a photocopy using the important document and placing coins in the photocopy machine. Use the picture to represent the photocopier. Motion for the learners to repeat.)
>
> **G:** "Copy."
>
> **I:** "Copy." (Mime making a copy. Motion for the learners to repeat.)
>
> **G:** "Copy."

2. Have learners repeat the verb at least three times.
3. Introduce **important** by holding up the various documents introduced in Oral Language Activity 1 (the pay stub and W-2).

4. Use money and a wallet to further demonstrate the term **important** to the group.
5. Use receipts or other unimportant pieces of paper to demonstrate that some papers are not important documents.

> **I:** "Important." (Hold up the W-2.)
> **I:** "W-2 is important. Important." (Motion for the group to repeat.)
> **G:** "Important."
> **I:** "Important." (Hold up the pay stub and place it on the W-2. Motion for the group to repeat.)
> **G:** "Important."
> **I:** "Important." (Hold up money and place it in a wallet. Motion for the group to repeat.)
> **G:** "Important."
> **I:** "Important?" (Hold up a grocery receipt.)
> **I:** "Important. No." (Hold up the **No** card.)
> **I:** "Important?" (Hold up the **W-2** card.)
> **I:** "Important. Yes." (Hold up the **Yes** card.)

NOTE

The **save** card from Unit 3 can also be used here.

6. Introduce **save** by using a manila folder or envelope in which to place the important documents.

> **I:** "Save." (Hold up a document and place it in the folder or envelope.)
> **I:** " Save." (Repeat the action of placing the document in the folder or envelope and motion for the group to respond.)
> **G:** "Save."

7. Have the group repeat each word at least three times.

Concept Development Activity

1. Gather all of the large noun cards and all of the realia (W-2s, pay stubs, money—including bills and coins, receipts, the wallet(s) or purse(s), etc.).
2. Mix the cards and realia and place the items on the table or other flat surface. Keep the manila folder(s) or envelope(s) separate.
3. Have the learners help sort the materials according to the appropriate category, identifying each term verbally.

Categories

money	pay stub
tax	W-2

4. Use the manila file folder(s) or envelope(s) to help illustrate the meaning of **save**.

5. Have the learners associate each material with the terms **important** and/**save.**

> **I:** "What's this?" (Hold up a pay stub. Motion for a response.)
>
> **G:** "Pay stub."
>
> **I:** "OK. Important?" (Ask the group for a response.)
>
> **G:** "Yes. Important."
>
> **I:** "Save?" (Demonstrate what might be done with the document. Mime crumpling it up, throwing it away, saving it in the envelope, etc. Wait a minute after giving the choices, then mime putting the document in the manila folder or envelope. Motion for a response.)
>
> **G:** "Yes. Save."
>
> **I:** "Good. Save pay stub." (Place the pay stub in the manila folder or envelope.)
>
> **I:** "Save pay stub." (Motion for the group to repeat.)
>
> **G:** "Save pay stub."

6. Repeat the procedure with other items, allowing the learners to decide what is important and how to save items.
7. Have the group associate putting money in a wallet or purse instead of a manila folder or envelope.
8. Use unimportant items (store or restaurant receipts, junk mail, scrap paper, etc.) to illustrate the difference between important items that need to be saved and items that do not need to be saved.
9. Ask the learners to repeat each word or phrase as much as possible to ensure verbal practice within the activity.
10. Repeat the activity as necessary to make sure that learners understand what documents are important and how they should be saved.

Comprehension Check

1. Distributea Comprehension Check activity sheet to each learner.
2. Ask learners to check documents that are important and should be saved for tax purposes.

> **I:** "Save?" (Point to the receipt from a supermarket. Motion for a response.)
>
> **G:** "No."
>
> **I:** " Important?" (Point to the receipt from a supermarket. Motion for a response.)
>
> **G:** "No."
>
> **I:** "Save? Important?" (Point to the W-2. Motion for a response.)
>
> **G:** "Yes."

paper with dollar amount listed
pay stub
paper with telephone number written on it
supermarket receipt
money
W-2

Oral Language Activity 4

MATERIALS

Large noun cards (two sets)

Large question card

Real or instructor-made replicas of a W-2, pay stub, and tax form

Real or play money

OK/Not OK cards

Locating the Tax Activity

1. Hold up each noun card and review the words with the group (**money, pay stub, tax,** and **W-2**).
2. Hold up cards or realia at random. Prompt learners to distinguish and identify each one.
3. Assist learners as necessary.

> **I:** "What's this?" (Hold up the **W-2** card or realia equivalent. Motion for a response.)
>
> **G:** "W-2."
>
> **I:** "Good. What's this?" (Hold up the **pay stub** card. Motion for a response.)
>
> **G:** "Pay stub."
>
> **I:** "Nice work. What's this?" (Hold up the **W-2** card. Circle the state income tax. Point to the tax circled. Motion for a response.)
>
> **G:** "Tax."
>
> **I:** "How much is it?" (Point to the circled amount.)
>
> **G:** "$607.62."
>
> **I:** "Great. What's this?" (Hold up the **pay stub** card with the federal tax circled. Motion for a response.)
>
> **G:** "Tax."
>
> **I:** "How much is it?" (Point to the circled amount.)
>
> **G:** "$88.20."
>
> **I:** "Great work!"

4. Continue to review, circling and pointing to other tax amounts and having learners identify them.

Matching the Tax Activity

1. Make two sets of the large noun cards, excluding the **money** card, for this activity. Circle approprieate tax amounts to create pairs
2. Shuffle the cards and place them picture-side down on a table or other available surface.

NOTE

Photocopy each set of cards on a different color of paper to facilitate the activity. If learners cannot remember a term, say it out loud and have the group repeat it.

3. Model the activity by choosing two cards, and show them to the group.
4. Ask the group to identify each picture and the tax amount circled.
5. Show the group one failure and one success in finding a matched pair.
6. Demonstrate how an individual can take another turn after finding a matched pair.
7. Draw two cards that will demonstrate an unmatched pair, as in the following example.

> **I:** " What's this?" (Hold up the **W-2** card and motion for a response.)
> **G:** "W-2."
> **I:** "What's this?" (Draw and hold up the **pay stub** card. Motion for a response.)
> **G:** "Pay stub."
> **I:** "No match."

8. Draw two cards that will demonstrate a matched pair, as in the following example. (Mark a matched pair of cards, if necessary, to ensure picking appropriate cards.)

> **I:** "What's this?" (Hold up the **W-2** card and motion for a response.)
> **G:** "W-2."
> **I:** "What's this?" (Hold up the other **W-2** card and motion for a response.)
> **G:** "W-2."
> **I:** "OK. Match."
> **I:** "How much is it?" (Point to the tax amount circled on each card. Motion for a response.)
> **G:** "$607.62."
> **I:** " OK. Match."

9. Assist learners as necessary with identifying documents and amounts of money.

Comprehension Check

1. Hold up two of the same document with matching dollar amounts clearly marked.
2. Ask learners if the pair is OK or Not OK based on whether the dollar amounts match.
3. Continue by holding up pairs of documents with matching or nonmatching dollar amounts. Prompt learners to respond with OK or Not OK.

> **I:** "Tax. How much is it?" (Hold up a document showing a tax amount. Point to the circled amount. Motion for a response.)
>
> **G:** "$10.28."
>
> **I:** "Good. What's this?" (Hold up another document with $10.28 circled. Motion for a response.)
>
> **G:** "Tax."
>
> **I:** "How much?" (Point to the circled amount. Motion for a response.)
>
> **G:** "$10.28."
>
> **I:** "Good. OK or Not OK?" (Hold up the **OK** and **Not OK** cards. Motion for a response.)
>
> **G:** "OK."

Reading Activity

MATERIALS

Large vocabulary cards

Document Matching activity sheet (one enlarged and one per learner)

Review

1. Shuffle the large vocabulary cards.
2. Show each card to the group while pronouncing each word slowly and clearly.
3. Run a finger under each word to help learners begin to recognize the words apart from the pictures.
4. Have the learners repeat the words at least three times.

> **I:** "W-2." (Point to the word.)
>
> **G:** "W-2."
>
> **I:** "W-2." (Underline the word with a finger. Motion for the group to repeat the word.)
>
> **G:** "W-2."

NOTE

Separating words from pictures should be done gradually and after plenty of practice.

5. Continue to review with the cards, using the pattern above.
6. Fold cards in half to show only the words, to help learners become less dependent on the pictures.
7. Move from group to individual practice as learners become more comfortable reading the words without the assistance of the pictures.

Document Matching Activity

1. Place the large vocabulary cards on the board or other visible surface to assist learners with the activity sheet.
2. Display an enlarged Document Matching activity sheet on the board or other visible surface.
3. Distribute a Document Matching activity sheet to each learner.

4. Model the activity using the enlarged activity sheet. Have learners identify each document by name.
5. Model for learners how to draw a line from each document to the corresponding word on the opposite side of the activity sheet.
6. Assist learners as necessary to complete their own activity sheets.

Writing Activity

MATERIALS

Large vocabulary cards

Writing Checklist activity sheet (one enlarged and one per learner)

Review

1. Shuffle the large vocabulary cards.
2. Show each card to the group while pronouncing each word slowly and clearly.
3. Run a finger under each word to help learners begin to recognize the words apart from the pictures.
4. Have the learners repeat the words at least three times.

> **I:** "Pay stub." (Point to the term.)
> **G:** "Pay stub."
> **I:** " Pay stub." (Underline the term with a finger. Motion for the group to repeat the term.)
> **G:** "Pay stub."

NOTE

Separating words from pictures should be done gradually and after plenty of practice.

5. Continue to review with the cards, using the pattern above.
6. Fold cards in half to show only the words, to help learners become less dependent on the pictures.
7. Move from group to individual practice as learners become more comfortable reading the words without the assistance of the pictures.

Checklist Activity

1. Display the large vocabulary cards on the board or other visible surface to assist learners with the activity sheet.
2. Display an enlarged Checklist activity sheet in a visible location. Demonstrate on the enlarged sheet how to complete the checklist.
3. Ask the learners to identify each picture. Model how to write the correct word next to each one.
4. Have learners complete their own checklists.
5. Assist learners as necessary.

Lesson B – Civic Responsibility

Income Tax

VOCABULARY

NOUNS

April 15th

ITIN (Individual Taxpayer Identification Number)

Tax form

PREPOSITIONS

After

Before

VERB

Mail

SENTENCE

I need _____.

Objectives

- To help learners understand what documents are necessary for filing taxes
- To ensure that learners understand the importance of filing income tax forms on time

Materials Included

- Storyboard
- Large reproducible vocabulary cards
- Comprehension Check activity sheet
- Storyboard Writing activity sheet
- **OK/Not OK** cards (page 180)
- **Yes/No** cards

Materials Needed

- Real or (preferably) instructor-made replicas of Social Security cards and ITIN forms
- Tax forms (1040EZ)
- Calendar page with April 15th marked
- A stamped and addressed envelope with letter
- Pictures of weather conditions (snowy, rainy, etc.) with corresponding pictures of weather-appropriate clothing
- Additional instructor copy (enlarged) of the activity sheets

Civics Introduction

Income Tax

Working individuals must report their earnings and tax withholdings to the Internal Revenue Service (IRS) each tax year by April 15th. Filing taxes requires an individual to obtain tax forms and to have a valid Social Security number or Individual Tax Identification Number (ITIN) and a W-2. Nonresident or resident aliens and other adults who are not eligible for a Social Security number but who are required to report income tax may obtain an ITIN from the IRS for the purpose of filing taxes with both federal and state governments. An ITIN may be used <u>only</u> for tax filing purposes and should not be used by individuals who have or are eligible for a valid Social Security number. The ITIN does not authorize work.[1]

Preparing for Tax Time is a topic of relevance to new arrivals who may not be aware of the income tax reporting requirements in the U.S. This unit is designed to inform newly arrived or any other non-English-speaking adults about income tax reporting and is not in any way a protocol for filing that tax. While filing income tax is a requirement for employees in the U.S., the content and documents used must be individualized according to a person's needs.

The consequences for not filing income tax vary greatly, depending on the legal status and the degree and type of fraud committed. Possible consequences may be deportation, fines, and/or a permanent ban on obtaining legal status to reside and work in the U.S.

[1]http://www.irs.gov/individuals/article/0,,id=96287,00.html
(viewed 9/14/05)

Storyboard Activity

MATERIALS

Storyboard

Introduce Storyboard

1. Hold up each storyboard frame and point to each picture.
2. Ask the learners to identify vocabulary in the pictures.
3. Point to the parts of each frame to elicit vocabulary.

> **I:** "What's this?" (Point to the mailbox. Motion for the learners to respond.)

4. Narrate the story using the following sentences:

> **Frame 1:** I need a W-2.
> **Frame 2:** I need an ITIN.
> **Frame 3:** I need a tax form.
> **Frame 4:** Mail taxes before April 15th.

5. Repeat the sentences that accompany the storyboard at least three times.

Oral Language Activity 1

MATERIALS

Large noun cards (from Lessons A & B)

Tax forms

Real or instructor-made replica of ITIN form

Calendar with April 15th marked

Pictures of weather conditions and weather-appropriate clothing

Yes/No cards

NOTE

An ITIN number can be issued for tax purposes only if the filer does not have or cannot obtain a valid Social Security number. **Social Security card** may be taught in addition to or in place of **ITIN** when applicable to the group.

Introduce Nouns and Sentence Form

1. Introduce target vocabulary terms to the group. Hold up the large vocabulary cards (**April 15th, tax form,** and **ITIN**) and say each term clearly.
2. Use realia and pictures as necessary to ensure that learners understand the vocabulary terms.

> **I:** "April 15th." (Hold up the **April 15th** card and point to the marked date on the calendar. Motion for the group to repeat together.)
> **G:** "April 15th."
> **I:** "Good. April 15th." (Motion for the group to repeat the date while pointing to it on the **April 15th** card.)
> **G:** "April 15th."
> **I:** "April 15th." (Motion for the group to repeat. Put the **April 15th** card at the front of the room.)
> **G:** "April 15th."

3. Introduce the remaining nouns using the format above (**tax form** and **ITIN).**
4. Use sample tax forms and other documents to help learners associate the target nouns with realia.
5. Say each term and have the group repeat each one three times.

6. Repeat any words more than three times as necessary.
7. Help learners understand the concept of **need** using weather conditions.
8. Hold up pictures of extreme weather (snow, rain, etc.) and associate each condition with weather-appropriate clothing.

> **I:** "It's snowing. I need a coat." (Hold up a picture of snowy weather. Hold up a picture of a coat.)
>
> **I:** "It's raining. I need an umbrella." (Hold up a picture of a rainy day. Hold up a picture of an umbrella.)
>
> **I:** "I need." (Motion for the group to repeat.)
>
> **G:** "I need."
>
> **I:** "I need." (Hold up a tax form and an ITIN.)
>
> **I:** "I need an ITIN." (Motion for the group to repeat.)
>
> **G:** "I need an ITIN.

9. Associate the concept of **need** with target vocabulary from Lessons A and B **(pay stub, W-2, tax form,** and **money).**
10. Substitute each item into the sentence, using the vocabulary cards or realia from Lessons A and B. Repeat the sentences at least three times.

Suggested Combinations

I need a pay stub.	I need a W-2.
I need a tax form.	I need money.

> **NOTE**
>
> Multiple sets of the large noun cards might be needed depending on the size of the group. Photocopy each set of cards on a different color of paper to facilitate the activity.

The *I Need* Activity

1. In a visible location, place a calendar with April 15th marked clearly.
2. Point to the date and elicit the correct date from the group.

> **I:** "What's this?" (Point to the date on the calendar. Motion for a response.)
>
> **G:** "April 15th."

3. Shuffle two or more sets of large noun cards (from Lessons A and B) together and model how to do the activity.
4. Pass out four cards to each learner.
5. Place the remaining cards in a pile facedown in the center of the group.
6. Motion for the learners to look at their cards.
7. Have each learner take a turn drawing a card from the pile, identifying the term on the card, and discarding unnecessary cards in the set being held. Continue until someone has the four items necessary for filing taxes.

> **NOTE**
>
> The object of the activity is to collect all four items that are necessary for filing taxes.

Items Needed for Filing Taxes

April 15th	Tax form
ITIN	W-2

8. Model the sentence pattern needed for this activity with one learner's cards.

> **L:** "W-2, ITIN, tax form. (Learner should show the **W-2, ITIN,** and **tax form** cards.)
>
> **I:** "What do you need?" (Show all three items and ask the learner to identify the item that is needed.)
>
> **L:** "I need April 15th." (Learner should identify the item that is missing from the group of four cards needed for filing taxes.)

9. Assist learners as necessary.

Comprehension Check

1. Reshuffle the large target vocabulary cards.
2. Hold up the cards, one by one, identifying the vocabulary correctly and incorrectly at random.
3. Model for the learners how to say Yes when the card is correctly identified, and No when it is incorrectly identified.
4. Use the **Yes/No** cards to clarify the appropriate response.

> **I:** "Tax form." (Hold up the **tax form** card.)
>
> **I:** "Tax form. Yes." (Point to the **tax form** card and nod in agreement. Hold up the **Yes** card. Motion for the learners to repeat.)
>
> **G:** "Yes."
>
> **I:** "W-2." (Hold up the **mail** card.)
>
> **I:** "W-2. No." (Point to the **mail** card and motion disagreement. Hold up the **No** card. Motion for the learners to repeat.)
>
> **G:** "No."

5. Continue to review the target vocabulary, repeating cards with correct or incorrect identification at random.
6. Repeat words as necessary.

Oral Language Activity 2

MATERIALS

Large verb card

Sample tax forms

Real or instructor-made replicas of W-2s, ITINs, and (if appropriate for group) Social Security cards

A calendar with April 15th marked

Storyboard

Introduce the Verb and Prepositions

1. Hold up the verb card and use pictures and realia to illustrate the verb **mail.**
2. Have the learners repeat the verb at least three times.

> **I:** "Mail." (Point to the letter and picture of the mailbox. Motion for learners to repeat.)
>
> **G:** "Mail."
>
> **I:** "Mail." (Point to the letter and picture of the mailbox. Motion for learners to repeat.)
>
> **G:** "Mail."
>
> **I:** "Mail." (Point to the letter and picture of the mailbox. Motion for learners to repeat.)
>
> **G:** "Mail."

3. Hold up the **April 15th** card and use the calendar with April 15th marked to illustrate the terms **before** and **after.**
4. Have the learners repeat each preposition at least three times.

> **I:** "Before." (Point to dates prior to April 15th on the calendar. Motion for learners to repeat.)
>
> **G:** "Before."
>
> **I:** "Before." (Point to dates prior to April 15th on the calendar. Motion for learners to repeat.)
>
> **G:** "Before."
>
> **I:** "Before." (Point to dates prior to April 15th on the calendar. Motion for learners to repeat.)
>
> **G:** "Before."

5. Repeat the above procedure with **after** by pointing to dates after April 15th.
6. Continue on to the activity when the group has a solid understanding of **before** and **after.**

Filing Taxes Storyboard Activity

1. Review the correct order of the storyboard by holding up each card in the proper order and saying the corresponding sentence clearly.

> **I:** "I need a W-2." (Show **Frame 1** and hold up the **W-2** card or realia.)
>
> **I:** "I need an ITIN." (Show **Frame 2** and hold up the **ITIN** card or realia.)
>
> **I:** "I need a tax form." (Show **Frame 3** and hold up the **tax form** card or realia.)
>
> **I:** "Mail taxes before April 15th." (Show **Frame 4** and hold up the **mail** and **April 15th** cards. Use the calendar to illustrate **before April 15th.)**

2. Have learners recite the storyboard as a group. Model each sentence and have learners repeat. Use the storyboard frames and realia to elicit responses.
3. Make sure learners repeat each word to ensure clear communication.
4. Shuffle the storyboard frames and place them at random on the table or other visible surface.
5. Ask learners to place them back in the correct order as a group.
6. Have learners repeat the sentence corresponding to each frame in order.
7. Assist learners as necessary.

Comprehension Check

1. Shuffle the vocabulary cards and realia that correspond to the storyboard.
2. Distribute the vocabulary cards and realia to the learners.
3. Hold up each frame in sequence and say the sentence that corresponds to each frame.
4. Ask the group to hold up the cards and realia that correspond to each storyboard frame. Motion for learners to repeat the target vocabulary item.

> **I:** "I need a W-2." (Motion for a response.)
>
> **G:** "W-2." (Learners should hold up a W-2 and the **W-2** card.)

5. Continue with other frames, eliciting a response from the learners. Have learners repeat the word and hold up the corresponding card and realia.

Oral Language Activity 3

Large vocabulary cards
(from Lessons A & B)

Instructor-provided
realia

OK/Not OK cards

Review Target Vocabulary

1. Review each target vocabulary term, using the large vocabulary cards and the corresponding realia.
2. Assist learners in identifying each term verbally.

> **I:** "What's this?" (Hold up the **ITIN** card. Motion for the group to respond.)
>
> **G:** "ITIN."
>
> **I:** "Great. What's this?" (Hold up the **April 15th** card. Motion for a response.)
>
> **G:** "April 15th."

3. Continue the review of target vocabulary, using the format above, with the large cards and corresponding realia.

Suggested Realia

April 15th—calendar

ITIN—example of an ITIN form

tax form—sample 1040EZ

before—calendar with dates marked before April 15th

after—calendar with dates marked after April 15th

mail—an addressed envelope containing tax forms, a picture of a mailbox

Find the Documents Activity

1. Mix the vocabulary cards**(April 15th, ITIN, W-2,** and **tax form)** and the corresponding realia.
2. Place the cards and documents faceup on the table or another visible surface.
3. Use verbal and visual prompts. Have learners choose both the card and item that correspond to the prompt. Ask them to hold up the card and item and repeat the term.

> **I:** "What do I need?" (Hold up the **W-2** card. Motion for the learners to find the corresponding card or realia.)
>
> **G:** "W-2." (Learners should hold up the **W-2** card or realia.)
>
> **I:** "What do I need?" (Hold up the **ITIN** card. Motion for the learners to find the corresponding card or realia.)
>
> **G:** "ITIN." (Learners should hold up the **ITIN** card or realia.)
>
> **I:** "What do I need?" (Hold up the **tax form** card. Motion for the learners to find the corresponding card or realia.)
>
> **G:** "Tax form." (Learners should hold up the **tax form** card or realia.)
>
> **I:** "What do I need?" (Hold up the **April 15th** card. Motion for the learners to find the corresponding card or realia.)
>
> **G:** "April 15th." (Learners should hold up the **April 15th** card or realia.)

4. Use the calendar to elicit target prepositions **before** and **after.**
5. Help learners associate OK or Not OK with having documents ready before April 15th versus after April 15th.

> **I:** "Mail before April 15th. OK or Not OK?" (Hold up the calendar and point to the dates prior to April 15th. Hold up the tax form or **tax form** card. Motion for the group to respond.)
>
> **G:** "OK."
>
> **I:** "Mail after April 15th. OK or Not OK?" (Hold up the calendar and point to the dates after April 15th. Hold up the tax form or **tax form** card. Motion for the group to respond.)
>
> **G:** "Not OK."

6. Repeat activity as necessary with varied realia or pictures (e.g., an envelope with tax forms or picture of a mailbox) and varied dates before or after April 15th, to ensure the group's comprehension of the process and concept of filing taxes.

Comprehension Check

1. Hold up two cards or a combination of a card and realia or picture. Ask learners to identify which card is necessary for filing taxes.

> **I:** "What do you need?" (Hold up a picture of rainy weather and the **tax form** card.)
>
> **G:** "Tax form." (Point to the **tax form** card.)

2. Repeat with various pairs and have learners choose the correct card, picture, or item.

3. Distribute **OK/Not OK** cards so that each learner has a set.
4. Hold up the cards or items that represent documents needed for filing taxes.
5. Ask learners to confirm when taxes should be mailed using the **OK** and **Not OK** cards.

> **I:** "Before April 15th. OK or Not OK?" (Hold up the envelope containing tax documents and point to the dates prior to April 15th on the calendar. Motion for a response.)
>
> **G:** "OK." (Learners should hold up the **OK** card.)
>
> **I:** "After April 15th. OK or Not OK?" (Hold up the envelope containing tax documents and point to the dates after April 15th on the calendar. Motion for a response.)
>
> **G:** "Not OK." (Learners should hold up the **Not OK** card.)

Oral Language Activity 4

Introduce the Dialogue

1. Write the dialogue (see example below) on the board or other available surface. Read it for the group, pointing to each word.
2. Place the large vocabulary cards and realia in a visible location at the front of the room to use for eliciting information.

> **Speaker 1:** "What do you need?" (Hold up the **W-2, ITIN,** and **tax form** cards. Motion for a response.)
>
> **Speaker 2:** "I need a W-2, ITIN, and tax form."
>
> **Speaker 1:** "What do you do?" (Hold up the **mail** card and motion for a response.)
>
> **Speaker 2:** "Mail tax form."
>
> **Speaker 1:** "When?" (Point to the dates prior to April 15th on the calendar. Motion for a response.)
>
> **Speaker 2:** "Before April 15th."

3. Point to each word whenever the dialogue is repeated in this activity.
4. Go through the dialogue, using appropriate cards and realia, with the instructor as speaker 1 and the group responding as Speaker 2.

MATERIALS

Large vocabulary cards

Storyboard

Comprehension Check activity sheet (one enlarged and one per learner)

NOTE

Social Security card can be used in addition to or in place of **ITIN** based on the needs of the group.

NOTE

Pairing learners with each other to perform the dialogue may be done to increase the difficulty level of the activity.

Dialogue Activity

1. Write the dialogue (see example below), on the board or other available surface. Read it for the group, pointing to each word.

> **Speaker 1:** "What do you need?" (Hold up the **W-2, ITIN,** and **tax form** cards. Motion for a response.)
>
> **Speaker 2:** "I need a W-2, ITIN, and tax form."
>
> **Speaker 1:** "What do you do?" (Hold up the **mail** card and motion for a response.)
>
> **Speaker 2:** "Mail tax form."
>
> **Speaker 1:** "When?" (Point to the dates prior to April 15th on the calendar. Motion for a response.)
>
> **Speaker 2:** "Before April 15th."

2. Point to each word whenever the dialogue is repeated in this activity.
3. Perform the dialogue together, with the instructor as Speaker 1 and the group responding to the questions and prompts as Speaker 2.
4. Perform the dialogue as a group three times, using the storyboard and realia as necessary to dramatize the dialogue.
5. Assist learners as needed.

Comprehension Check

1. Distribute a Comprehension Check activity sheet to each learner.
2. Place an enlarged activity sheet in a visible location in the room to assist the group.
3. Perform the Speaker 1 portion of the dialogue to prompt learners.
4. Point to each choice. Ask the learners to respond verbally and circle the correct response.

NOTE

Correct responses are based on the dialogue in Oral Language Activity 4.

> **I:** "What do you need?" (Point to the two choices—tax form or grocery receipt. Motion for a response.)
>
> **G:** "Tax form." (Learners should point to the tax form picture.)
>
> **I:** "What do you do?" (Point to the two choices—throw away or mail tax form. Motion for a response.)
>
> **G:** "Mail tax form." (Learners should point to the mail picture.
>
> **I:** "When?" (Point to the two choices—after and before April 15th. Motion for a response.)
>
> **G:** "Before April 15th." (Learners should point to the picture showing dates before April 15th.)

Reading Activity

MATERIALS

Large vocabulary cards (from Lessons A & B; multiple sets if necessary)

Review

1. Shuffle all of the large vocabulary cards together.
2. Show each card to the group while pronouncing each word slowly and clearly.
3. Run a finger under each word to help learners begin to recognize the words apart from the pictures.
4. Have the learners repeat the words at least three times.

> **I:** "Mail." (Point to the word.)
> **G:** "Mail."
> **I:** "Mail." (Underline the word with a finger. Motion for the group to repeat the word.)
> **G:** "Mail."

NOTE

Separating words from pictures should be done gradually and after plenty of practice.

5. Continue to review with the cards, using the pattern above.
6. Fold cards in half to show only the words, to help learners become less dependent on the pictures.
7. Move from group to individual practice as learners become more comfortable reading the words without the assistance of the pictures.

Match the Pictures with the Words Activity

1. Cut a set of large vocabulary cards into picture and word cards and shuffle the picture and word cards separately.
2. Display the word cards on surfaces throughout the room.
3. Distribute pictures evenly among the learners.
4. Have learners stand up and move around the room to match each picture with the corresponding word card displayed.
5. Have learners say each vocabulary term after each match has been correctly identified.

NOTE

Learners can work individually or in pairs to find the word cards that correspond to the picture cards. Multiple sets of large vocabulary cards may be needed to give each learner or pair of learners a picture.

Writing Activity

MATERIALS

Large vocabulary cards (from Lessons A & B)

Storyboard Writing activity sheet

Review

1. Shuffle all of the large vocabulary cards together.
2. Show each card to the group while pronouncing each word slowly and clearly.
3. Run a finger under each word to help learners begin to recognize the words apart from the pictures.
4. Have the learners repeat the words at least three times.

> **I:** "Mail." (Point to the word.)
>
> **G:** "Mail."
>
> **I:** "Mail." (Underline the word with a finger. Motion for the group to repeat the word.)
>
> **G:** "Mail."

5. Continue to review with the cards, using the pattern above.
6. Fold cards in half to show only the words, to help learners become less dependent on the pictures.
7. Move from group to individual practice as learners become more comfortable reading the words without the assistance of the pictures.

Storyboard Writing Activity

1. Use the storyboard frames to review the correct order of filing taxes with the group.

Storyboard Frames

1: I need a W-2.   *3:* I need a tax form.
2: I need an ITIN.   *4:* Mail taxes before April 15th.

2. Display the storyboard in the correct order for the group to use as a reference.
3. Distribute a Storyboard Writing activity sheet to each learner.
4. Use an enlarged version of the activity sheet in a visible location in the room to demonstrate to learners how to complete the sheet.
5. Have learners identify each frame.
6. Motion for learners to complete the sentence for each frame on their own activity sheets, using the large displayed cards as a reference.
7. Assist learners as necessary.

4 Unit Review Activity

MATERIALS

Unit Review activity sheet (one enlarged and one per learner)

Large vocabulary cards (from Lessons A and B)

NOTE

The Unit Review Activity can be done as a group activity for reinforcing the concepts learned in the lesson or done as an individual activity for assessment purposes.

Check Yes or No Activity

1. Use the large vocabulary cards from LessonsA and B to review the vocabulary and concepts from the unit.
2. For review, ask learners if the documents are needed for tax time. Have learners respond Yes or No for each document.
3. Distribute a copy of the Unit Review activity sheet to each learner. Post an enlarged copy of the activity sheet in the front of the room.
4. Ask learners to complete the activity. If necessary, use the enlarged activity sheet to model checking Yes for the documents that they need for tax time and No for the documents that they don't need.

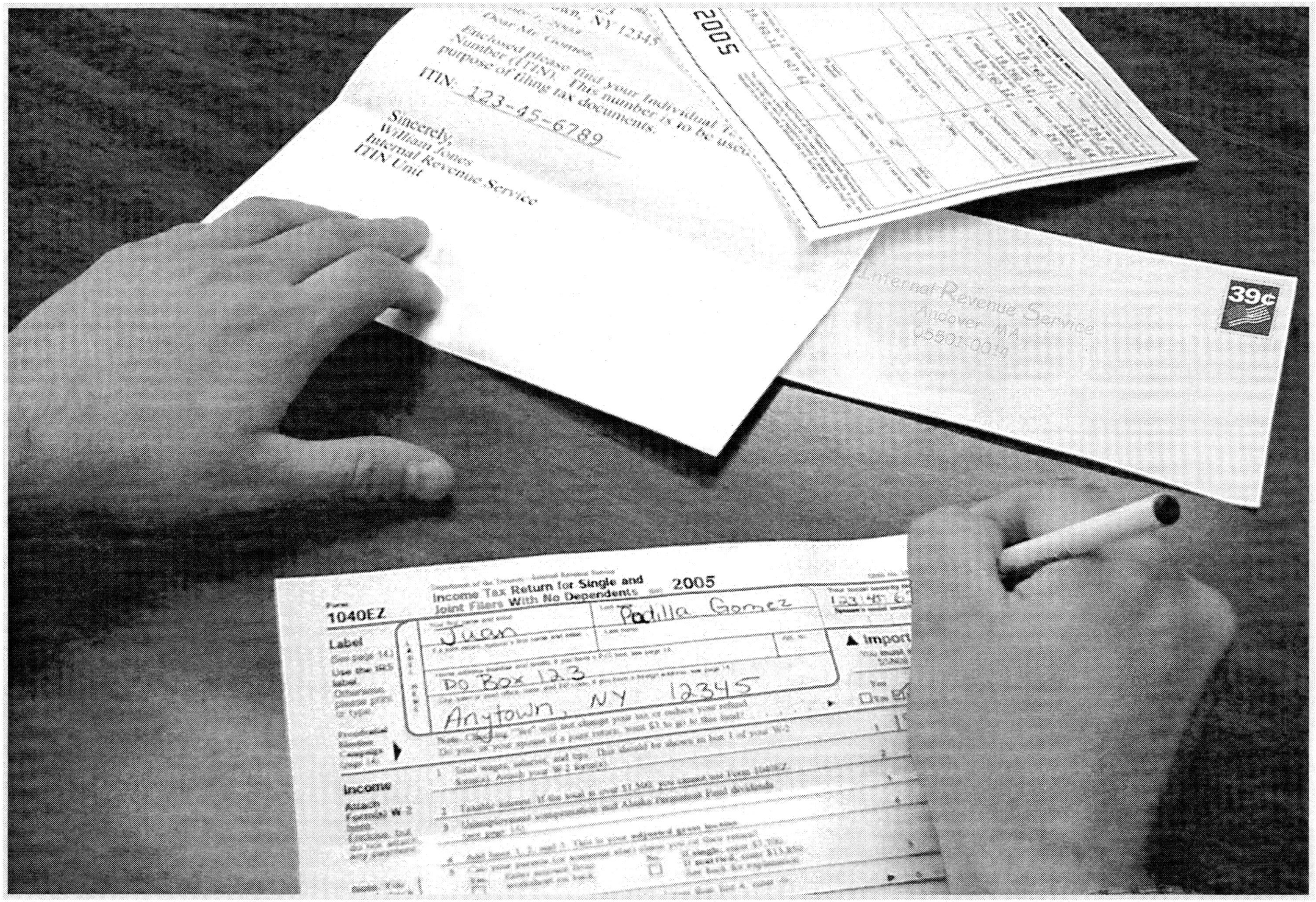
NY 12345
Dear Mr. Gomez,
Enclosed please find your Individual Ta
Number (ITIN). This number is to be used
purpose of filing tax documents.
ITIN: 123-45-6789
Sincerely,
William Jones
Internal Revenue Service
ITIN Unit
2005
Internal Revenue Service
Andover, MA
05501-0014
39¢
Form 1040EZ
Income Tax Return for Single and
Joint Filers With No Dependents
2005
Label
Juan
Padilla Gomez
PO Box 123
Anytown, NY 12345
Income

Money

Pay stub

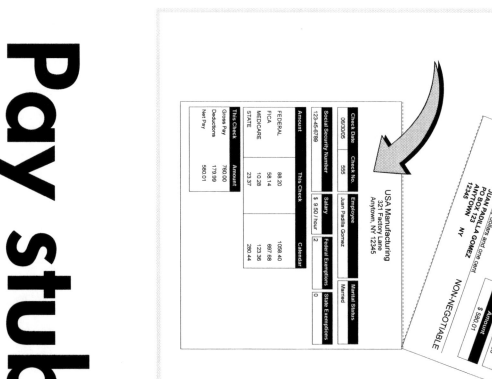

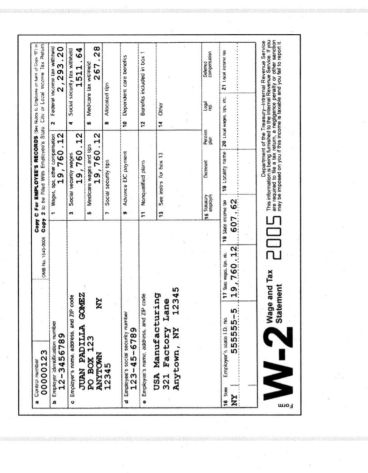

W-2

Tax

How much is it?

Unit 4 *Preparing for Tax Time:* A

Large Vocabulary Cards

Yes

No

Comprehension Check Activity

Check the documents that are important to save for tax time.

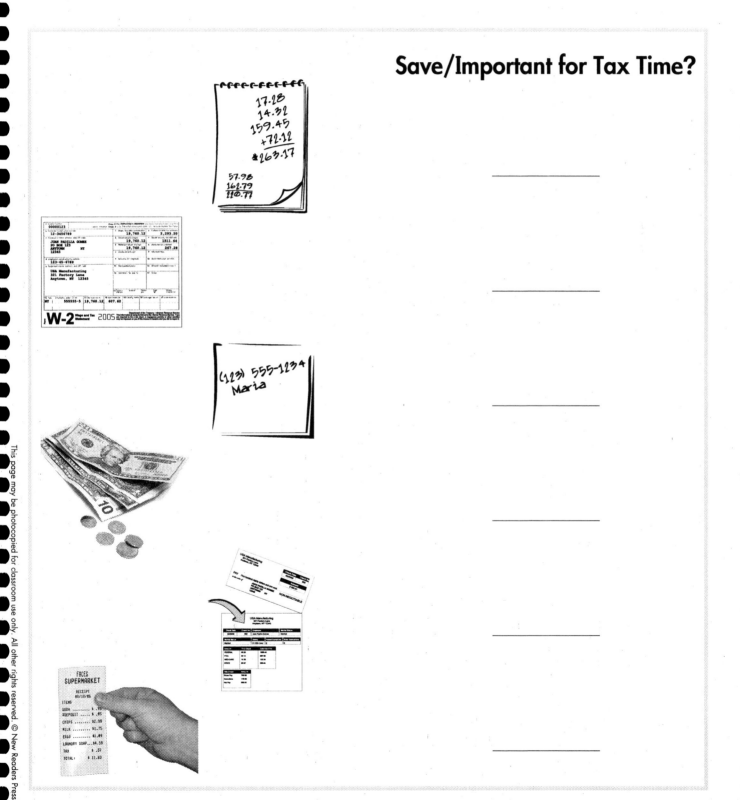

Save/Important for Tax Time?

_____

_____

_____

_____

_____

_____

Document Matching Activity

Draw a line to match the pictures with the words.

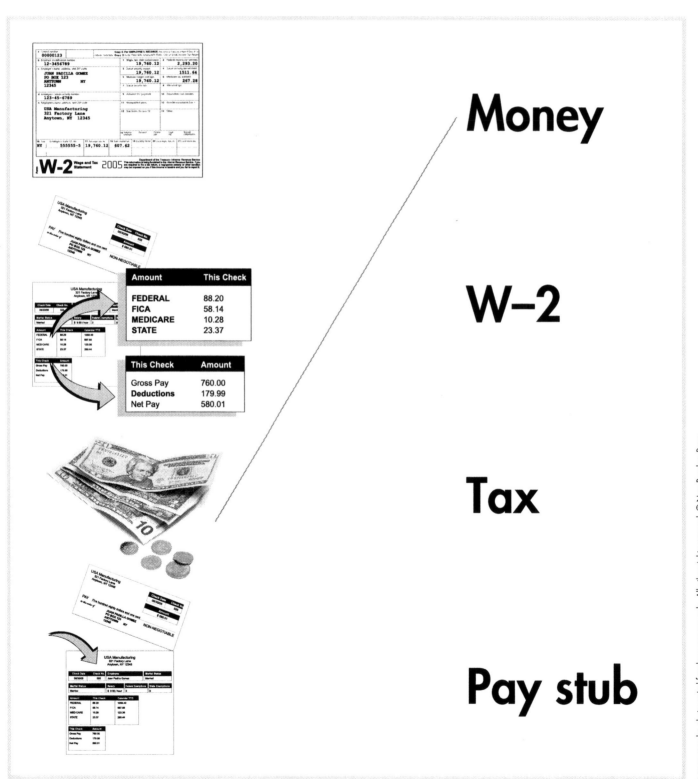

Money

W–2

Tax

Pay stub

Checklist Activity

Write the correct word next to each picture.

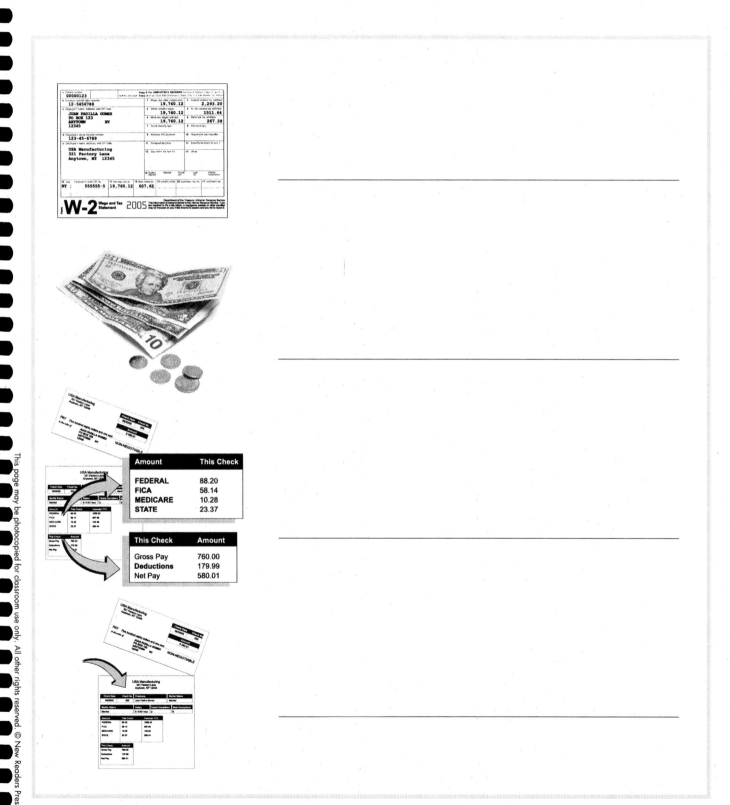

_____

_____

_____

_____

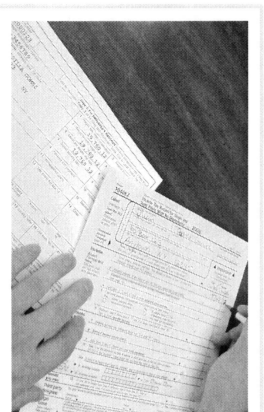

Storyboard Frame 3

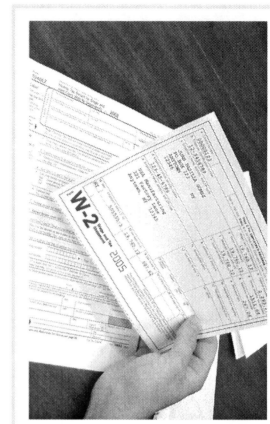

Storyboard Frame 1

Storyboard Frame 4

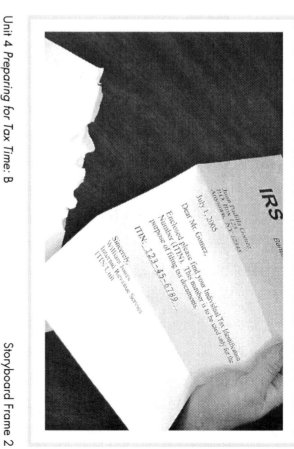

Storyboard Frame 2

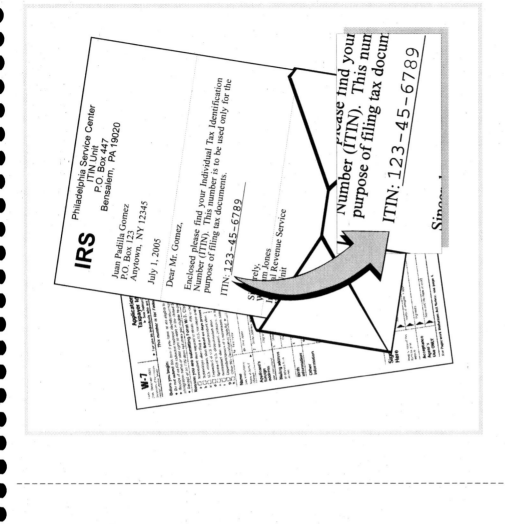

ITIN

(Individual Taxpayer Identification Number)

Unit 4 *Preparing for Tax Time:* B

✂

April 15th

Unit 4 *Preparing for Tax Time:* B

Tax form

Mail

Comprehension Check Activity

Listen to the instructor. Circle the picture that matches
the process of filing income tax forms.

Instructor asks . . .   ## Circle the correct picture

"What do you need?"

"What do you do?"

 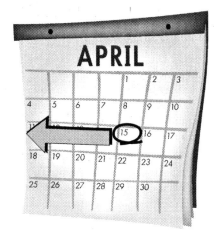

"When?"

Unit 4 *Preparing for Tax Time* Lesson B *Civic Responsibility*   Activity Sheet

Storyboard Writing Activity

Complete the sentence for each storyboard frame.

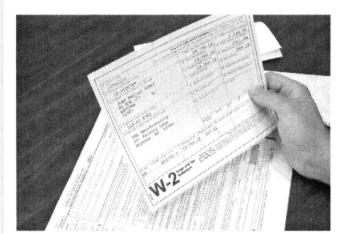

I need a _____.

I need an _____.

I need a _____.

_____ taxes _____ _____ _____.

Check Yes for the items needed for tax time. Check No for the items not needed.

Tax form

Yes ☐

No ☐

Money

Yes ☐

No ☐

ITIN

Yes ☐

No ☐

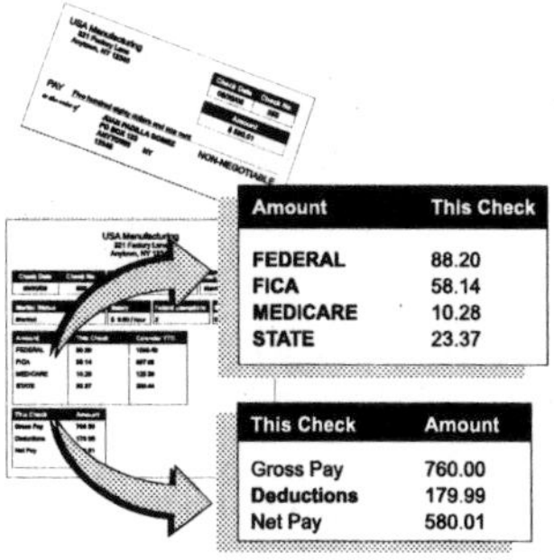

Tax

Yes ☐

No ☐

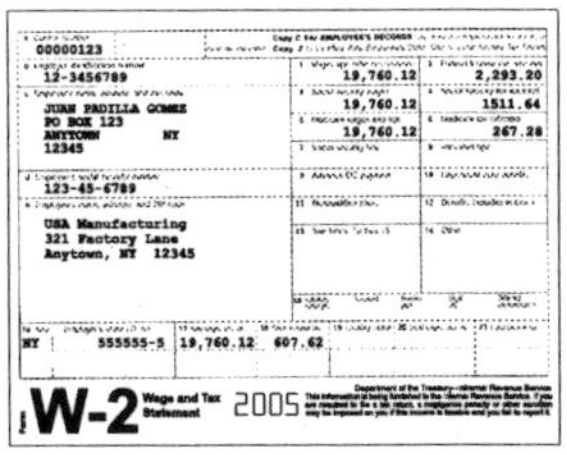

W–2

Yes ☐

No ☐

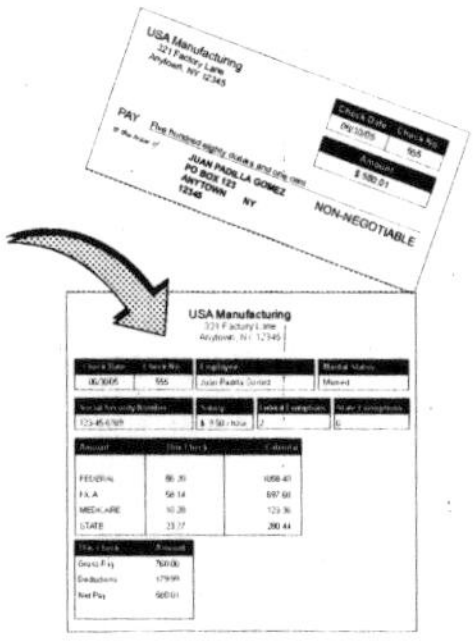

Pay stub

Yes ☐

No ☐

Mail before April 15th

Yes ☐

No ☐

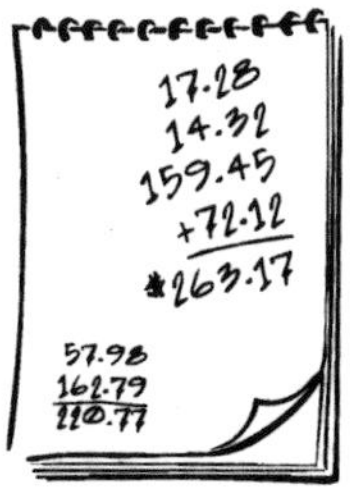

Scrap paper

Yes ☐

No ☐

Unit 4 *Preparing for Tax Time*

Unit Review Activity

OK

Not OK